Peter Roe Series XXIII

Translating and Illustrating Tolkien

Proceedings of The Tolkien Society
Autumn Seminar 2021

Edited by Will Sherwood

First published 2023 by Luna Press Publishing, Edinburgh
www.lunapresspublishing.com
Revised Edition 2024

ISBN-13: 978-1-915556-28-8

Contents

About the Peter Roe Memorial Fund

The Tolkien Society's seminar proceedings and other booklets are typically published under the auspices of the Peter Roe Memorial Fund, a fund in the Society's accounts that commemorates a young member who died in a traffic accident. Peter Roe, a young and very talented person joined the Society in 1979, shortly after his sixteenth birthday. He had discovered Middle-earth some time earlier, and was so inspired by it that he even developed his own system of runes, similar to the Dwarvish Angerthas, but which utilised logical sound values, matching the logical shapes of the runes. Peter was also an accomplished cartographer, and his bedroom was covered with multi-coloured maps of the journeys of the fellowship, plans of Middle-earth, and other drawings.

Peter was also a creative writer in both poetry and prose—the subject being incorporated into his own *Dwarvish Chronicles*. He was so enthusiastic about having joined the Society that he had written a letter ordering all the available back issues, and was on his way to buy envelopes when he was hit by a speeding lorry outside his home.

Sometime later, Jonathan and Lester Simons (at that time Chairman and Membership Secretary respectively) visited Peter's parents to see his room and to look at the work on which he had spent so much care and attention in such a tragically short life. It was obvious that Peter had produced, and would have continued to produce, material of such a high standard as to make a complete booklet, with poetry, calligraphy, stories and cartography. The then committee set up a special account in honour of Peter, with the consent of his parents, which would be the source of finance for the Society's special publications. Over the years a number of members have made generous donations to the fund.

The first publication to be financed by the Peter Roe Memorial Fund was *Some Light on Middle-earth* by Edward Crawford, published in 1985. Subsequent publications have been composed from papers delivered at Tolkien Society workshops and seminars, talks from guest speakers at the Annual Dinner, and collections of the best articles from past issues of *Amon Hen*, the Society's bulletin.

Dwarvish Fragments, an unfinished tale by Peter, was printed in *Mallorn* 15 (September 1980). A standalone collection of Peter's creative endeavours is currently being prepared for publication.

The Peter Roe Series

I — *Some Light on Middle-earth*, ed. by Edward Crawford (Pinner: The Tolkien Society, 1985)

II — *Leaves from the Tree: Tolkien's Short Fiction*, ed. by Trevor Reynolds (London: The Tolkien Society, 1991)

III — *The First and Second Ages*, ed. by Trevor Reynolds (London: The Tolkien Society, 1992; Edinburgh: Luna Press Publishing 2020)

IV — *Travel and Communication in Tolkien's Worlds*, ed. by Richard Crawshaw (Swindon: The Tolkien Society, 1996)

V — *Digging Potatoes, Growing Trees: Volume One*, ed. by Helen Armstrong (Swindon: The Tolkien Society, 1997)

VI — *Digging Potatoes, Growing Trees: Volume Two*, ed. by Helen Armstrong (Telford: The Tolkien Society, 1998)

VII — *Tolkien, the Sea and Scandinavia*, ed. by Richard Crawshaw (Telford: The Tolkien Society, 1999; Edinburgh: Luna Press Publishing, 2021)

VIII — *The Ways of Creative Mythologies*, ed. by Maria Kuteeva, 2 vols (Telford: The Tolkien Society, 2000)

IX — *Tolkien: A Mythology for England?*, ed. by Richard Crawshaw (Telford: The Tolkien Society, 2000)

X — *The Best of Amon Hen: Part One*, ed. by Andrew Wells, (Telford: The Tolkien Society, 2000)

XI — *Digging Potatoes, Growing Trees: Volume Three*, ed. by Helen Armstrong (Telford: The Tolkien Society, 2001)

XII — *Sindarin Lexicon*, Kenneth Chaij (Telford: The Tolkien Society, 2001)

XIII *The Best of Amon Hen: Part Two*, ed. by Andrew Wells (Telford: The Tolkien Society, 2002)

XIV *Tolkien: Influenced and Influencing*, ed. by Matthew Vernon (Telford: The Tolkien Society, 2005)

XV *Freedom, Fate and Choice in Middle-earth*, ed. by Christopher Kreuzer (London: The Tolkien Society, 2012)

XVI *Journeys & Destinations*, ed. by Ian Collier (Wolverhampton: The Tolkien Society, 2015)

XVII *Death and Immortality in Middle-earth*, ed. by Daniel Helen (Edinburgh: Luna Press Publishing, 2017)

XVIII *Poetry and Song in the works of J.R.R. Tolkien*, ed. by Anna Milon (Edinburgh: Luna Press Publishing, 2018)

XIX *Tolkien the Pagan? Reading Middle-earth through a spiritual lens*, ed. by Anna Milon (Edinburgh: Luna Press Publishing, 2019).

XX *Adapting Tolkien*, ed. by Will Sherwood (Edinburgh, Luna Press Publishing, 2021)

XXI *Twenty-First Century Receptions of Tolkien*, ed. by Will Sherwood (Edinburgh, Luna Press Publishing, 2022)

XXII *Tolkien and Diversity*, ed. by Will Sherwood (Edinburgh, Luna Press Publishing 2023)

Abbreviations

A&I	*The Lay of Aotrou and Itroun*, ed. by Verlyn Flieger (London: HarperCollins, 2016)
Arthur	*The Fall of Arthur*, ed. by Christopher Tolkien (London: HarperCollins, 2013; Boston: Houghton Mifflin Harcourt, 2013)
AW	*Ancrene Wisse* (Oxford: Oxford University Press, 1962)
B&L	*Beren and Lúthien*, ed. by Christopher Tolkien (London: HarperCollins, 2017)
Beowulf	*Beowulf: A Translation and Commentary, together with Sellic Spell*, ed. by Christopher Tolkien (London: HarperCollins, 2014; Boston: Houghton Mifflin Harcourt, 2014)
Bombadil	*The Adventures of Tom Bombadil and other verses from the Red Book* (London: George Allen & Unwin, 1962; Boston: Houghton Mifflin, 1962)
CoH	*The Children of Húrin*, ed. by Christopher Tolkien (London: HarperCollins, 2007; Boston: Houghton Mifflin Harcourt, 2007)
Exodus	*The Old English Exodus*, ed. by Joan Turville-Petre (Oxford: Oxford University Press, 1982)
Father Christmas	*Letters from Father Christmas*, ed. by Baillie Tolkien (London: George Allen & Unwin, 1976; Boston: Houghton Mifflin, 1976)

FoG	*The Fall of Gondolin*, ed. by Christopher Tolkien (London: HarperCollins, 2018).
FR	*The Fellowship of the Ring*
Hobbit	*The Hobbit*
Jewels	*The War of the Jewels,* ed. by Christopher Tolkien (London: HarperCollins, 1994; Boston: Houghton Mifflin, 1994)
Kullervo	*The Story of Kullervo,* ed. by Verlyn Flieger (London: HarperCollins, 2015; Boston: Houghton Mifflin Harcourt, 2016)
Lays	*The Lays of Beleriand,* ed. by Christopher Tolkien (London: George Allen & Unwin, 1985; Boston: Houghton Mifflin, 1985)
Letters	*The Letters of J.R.R. Tolkien,* ed. by Humphrey Carpenter with the assistance of Christopher Tolkien (London: George Allen & Unwin, 1981; Boston: Houghton Mifflin, 1981)
Lost Road	*The Lost Road and Other Writings*, ed. by Christopher Tolkien (London: Unwin Hyman, 1987; Boston: Houghton Mifflin, 1987)
Lost Tales I	*The Book of Lost Tales, Part One,* ed. by Christopher Tolkien (London: George Allen & Unwin, 1983; Boston: Houghton Mifflin, 1984)
Lost Tales II	*The Book of Lost Tales, Part Two*, ed. by Christopher Tolkien (London: George Allen & Unwin, 1984; Boston: Houghton Mifflin, 1984)

Monsters	*The Monsters and the Critics and Other Essays* (London: George Allen & Unwin, 1983; Boston: Houghton Mifflin, 1984)
Morgoth	*Morgoth's Ring*, ed. by Christopher Tolkien (London: HarperCollins, 1993; Boston: Houghton Mifflin, 1993)
OFS	*Tolkien On Fairy-stories*, ed. by Verlyn Flieger and Douglas A. Anderson (London: HarperCollins, 2008)
P&S	*Poems and Stories* (London: George Allen & Unwin, 1980; Boston: Houghton Mifflin, 1994)
Peoples	*The Peoples of Middle-earth*, ed. by Christopher Tolkien (London: HarperCollins, 1996; Boston: Houghton Mifflin, 1996)
Perilous Realm	*Tales from the Perilous Realm* (London: HarperCollins, 1997)
RK	*The Return of the King*
Silmarillion	*The Silmarillion*, ed. by Christopher Tolkien (London: George Allen & Unwin, 1977; Boston: Houghton Mifflin, 1977).
Sauron	*Sauron Defeated*, ed. by Christopher Tolkien (London: HarperCollins, 1992; Boston: Houghton Mifflin, 1992)
Secret Vice	*A Secret Vice: Tolkien on Invented Languages*, ed. by Dimitra Fimi and Andrew Higgins (London: HarperCollins, 2016)

Shadow	*The Return of the Shadow*, ed. by Christopher Tolkien (London: Unwin Hyman, 1988; Boston: Houghton Mifflin, 1988)
Shaping	*The Shaping of Middle-earth*, ed. by Christopher Tolkien (London: George Allen & Unwin, 1986; Boston: Houghton Mifflin, 1986)
S&G	*The Legend of Sigurd and Gudrún*, ed. by Christopher Tolkien (London: HarperCollins, 2009; Boston: Houghton Mifflin Harcourt, 2009)
TL	*Tree and Leaf*, 2nd edn (London: Unwin Hyman, 1988; Boston: Houghton Mifflin, 1989)
TT	*The Two Towers*
Treason	*The Treason of Isengard*, ed. by Christopher Tolkien (London: Unwin Hyman; Boston: Houghton Mifflin, 1989)
UT	*Unfinished Tales of Númenor and Middle-earth*, ed. by Christopher Tolkien (London: George Allen & Unwin, 1980; Boston: Houghton Mifflin, 1980)
War	*The War of the Ring*, ed. by Christopher Tolkien (London: Unwin Hyman, 1990; Boston: Houghton Mifflin, 1990)

Introduction

Will Sherwood

> "The translation of The Lord of the Rings will prove a formidable task, and I do not see how it can be performed satisfactorily without the assistance of the author. That assistance I am prepared to give, promptly, if I am consulted." (*Letters*, Letter 188, 248-9)

> "If a story says 'he climbed a hill and saw a river in the valley below,' the illustrator may catch, or nearly catch, his own vision of such a scene; but every hearer of the words will have his own picture, and it will be made out of all the hills and rivers and dales he has ever seen." (*OFS*, 82)

Translation

It is well-known amongst J.R.R. Tolkien's readers that when he was writing *The Lord of the Rings* (1954-1955), he conceived of the book (as well as *The Hobbit* 1937 and 'The Silmarillion') as a text that he had 'discovered', translated, and modernised for a twentieth-century audience. The appendix confirms this thesis:

> In presenting the matter of the Red Book, as a history for people of today to read, the whole of the linguistic setting has been translated as far as possible into terms of our own times. Only the languages alien to the Common Speech have

> been left in their original form; but these appear mainly in the names of persons and places. (*RK*, Appendix F, II, 1133)

Translation and the meaning that is transferred, lost, or created through it, is at the very heart of Tolkien's world-building. But this conceit originated with Tolkien's earliest narrative framework: *The Book of Lost Tales* (1910s-1930s), not with *The Lord of the Rings*. The work documented the myths and tales of the Fairies told to Eriol. Although the chain may present itself more so as just the result of the oral tradition being converted through textual transmission, such stories required translating before Eriol could disseminate them.

Besides his fictional works, Tolkien translated a significant number of medieval texts and was intimately familiar with the challenges the translator faced - offering his assistance on one occasion (see the epigram above). Tolkien himself described the translation of *The Lord of the Rings* as a "formidable task" and, as will be seen in this volume, translating his works ignites a host of questions regarding Tolkien's application of nomenclature, pronouns, lore and mythical backstory just to name a few. Translators are presented with the challenge of staying true to Tolkien's original text while adapting his writing using the grammatical structures of the target language - some abandoning or ignoring one to be successful with the other. Additionally, the act of translation posits the translator as a keyholder who can reshape meaning in accordance with the translator's personal beliefs or their broader culture. The result can be a recontextualised rendition that matches a particular ideology at a specific time in a culture's history. As is evidenced in this volume, it is common for translations of Tolkien's works to be critically analysed for their oversights when navigating the tricky waters that is the art of translation.

Illustration

Similar to Tolkien's self-imposed role as the 'founder' and 'translator' of Middle-earth, he heavily illustrated his own work, frequently visualising geography such as Shelob's lair in order to more accurately depict Arda. HarperCollins' recent 'Illustrated by the Author' series (*The Lord of the Rings* 2021, *The Silmarillion* 2022, *The Hobbit* 2023) powerfully elucidates Tolkien's proclivity for illustration as an integral component of world-building. It is an oft-told tale that he lovingly and painstakingly created three pages from the Book of Mazarbul for the publication of *The Fellowship of the Ring*, for them to be denied.[1]

An illustrator of his own work, Tolkien had a keen eye for the visual representation of a text. He admired the work of illustrators such as Pauline Baynes, Cor Blok, and Ingahild Grathmer (the Queen of Denmark) and others who illustrated versions of his texts. He was sensitive to the power of illustration which is evident by his compliments of Pauline Baynes's "wonderful pictures with a touch of 'fantasy', but primarily bright and clear visions of things that one might really see" (*Letters*, Letter 235, 312). Given Tolkien's reliance on illustration to guide the reader and reinforce the author's or the illustrator's vision, his earlier comments from 'On Fairy-stories' characteristically reflect his contradictory nature.[2]

1. For further background on the Book of Mazarbul see Dimitra Fimi's 'The Past as an Imaginary World: The Case of Medievalism (Chatterton, Tolkien, Eco)' http://dimitrafimi.com/the-past-as-an-imaginary-world-the-case-of-medievalism-chatterton-tolkien-eco/ and my own 'Tolkien and the Age of Forgery: Improving Antiquarian Practices in Arda in *Journal of Tolkien Research* 11.1 (2020).
2. See Verlyn Flieger's 'The Arch and the Keystone' in *Mythlore* 38.1 (2019).

Tolkien was acutely aware (although he did not always express it) that the audience was a pivotal creator of meaning: "every hearer of the words will have his own picture, and it will be made out of all the hills and rivers and dales he has ever seen". This reinforces the Foreword to the second edition of *The Lord of the Rings* where he emphasised the importance of applicability as the "freedom of the reader" (*FR*, 'Foreword to the Second Edition', xxiv). Tolkien's message is clear: each reader will possibly bring a different meaning to the artistic product that the author did not intend.

In the years following the publication of Tolkien's works, illustrators and artists have flocked eagerly to depict characters and scenarios from his stories. Consistently, artists have showcased their ability to bring new meaning, exploring and interrogating the text to elicit fresh visions of Arda.

Of the eleven papers, six are presented in this proceedings. Reflecting its own theme, *Translating and Illustrating Tolkien* continues the new approach that *Tolkien and Diversity* initiated by inviting authors to publish papers in English and their own language, thereby celebrating the multilingualism of the Tolkien community. Eric Reinders opens this volume by exploring how three Chinese translations handle the ambiguity of man-as-human and man-as-male, seeing the translations as stories instead of losses. Helena Real follows by addressing issues in Rubén Masera and Luis Domènech Spanish translation of *The Silmarillion*, offering solutions that align with Tolkien's original text. Next, Martha Celis Mendoza and Aline Esperanza Maza Vázquez turn our attention to a text often overlooked in Tolkien scholarship: *Roverandom*; they illuminate the ways in which the different descriptions of the characters, creatures, and nature itself are rendered into Spanish. Sonali Arvind Chunodkar follows by discussing how Mugdha Karnik's *Swami*

Mudrikancha (the Marathi translation of *The Lord of the Rings*) presents itself as a unique descendant of the Marathi mythic fiction genre. The penultimate paper by Joel Merriner builds on his *Tolkien and Diversity* (2023) paper by examining the use of motif borrowing and dislocation in Soviet Bloc illustrations for *The Lord of the Rings*. Marie Bretagnolle concludes the proceedings with an investigation into how questions of translation can meet questions of illustration and map-making, in order to see how one can (directly or indirectly) influence the other.

On behalf of the Tolkien Society, I would like to extend my deepest gratitude to the presenters of the Tolkien Society 2021 Autumn Seminar, without whom the event would not have happened. I would also like to thank the Society's committee for their continued support and guidance in the planning and running of the event, and the publishing of this proceedings. The publication itself is made possible by the generosity of the Peter Roe Memorial Fund, for which I am grateful.

The video for each talk is available on the Tolkien Society's YouTube channel here: https://youtube.com/playlist?list=PLoyx2jXs6Le922Pri2oonRMTfVg6V5oC4.

Bibliography

Tolkien. J.R.R., *The Letters of J.R.R. Tolkien*, ed. by Humphrey Carpenter with the assistance of Christopher Tolkien (London: HarperColllins, 2005).

—, *Tolkien On Fairy-stories*, ed. by Verlyn Flieger and Douglas A. Anderson (London: HarperCollins, 2008).

—, *The Lord of the Rings*, (London: HarperCollins, 2010).

The Problem of Éowyn's 'no living man am I' in three Chinese translations

Eric Reinders

As part of a project on the intersections of religion, fantasy, and translation, with a specific case study of reading Tolkien in Chinese, three translations of *The Lord of the Rings* will be examined in this paper: (1) in simplified characters for the China market by three translators (Ding Di 丁棣, Yao Jinrong 姚锦镕, Tang Dingjiu 汤定九) for the Yilin Press (2001) which for clarity's sake (and in accord with Chinese fan usage) will be referred to by the Press name; (2) in traditional characters for the Taiwan market by Zhu Xueheng 朱學恆 (Linking 2001); and (3) in simplified characters for the China market by Taiwan-based translator Deng Jiawan 邓嘉宛/鄧嘉宛 (Wenjing 2013).

Along with Elves and trolls and Ents, *The Lord of the Rings* references a strange creature we can all agree exists in the real world, namely human beings, or, as Tolkien calls them, "Men." Obviously this usage, "man" or "men" when referring to human beings in general, now feels very dated - although outside of the academy it isn't quite dated enough. The 1970s and 80s saw an uptick in resistance to this androcentrism. It would be hard to imagine Jacob Bronowski's *The Ascent of Man* (1973) being produced by the BBC today, and Huston Smith's 1958 *The Religions of Man* became *The World's Religions* in its revised edition of 1991. Nonetheless, when we read older books which talk about "Man" this and "Men" that, we have to do some mental editing. Tolkien belonged not only to an age but also a social world in which this androcentric usage was pervasive.

He has Elrond say, for example, "Farewell, and may the blessing of Elves and Men and all Free Folk go with you" (*FR*, 'The Ring Goes South', 274). For "Men," all three Chinese translations of this line give *renlei* 人類 (humankind, a gender-neutral term). Clearly, from the context and the capital-M, we know Elrond cannot mean the blessing of all Elves of any gender but only male people. The Chinese language is certainly capable of encoding patriarchy, but in this particular case it does not. Yet not all uses of "Man" in *The Lord of the Rings* are quite so easily gender-neutralized. Indeed, one of the key plot points of the whole story hinges on the androcentric ambiguity of "Man."

One of the fundamental differences between Chinese and English is that English, being alphabetic, has capital letters, and Chinese, being logographic, does not. This is not a trivial difference. Our text itself problematizes the upper and lower cases. When Gandalf introduces Pippin to the people of Gondor, he says: "His name is Peregrin, a very valiant man." The soldier Ingold asks, "Man?" And Pippin replies: "Man! […] Man! Indeed not! I am a hobbit" (*RK*, 'Minas Tirith', 733). Gandalf seems to be using "man" to mean male person. He might have said, "a very valiant fellow." But Ingold takes "man" to mean "human" and questions it; Pippin reads "man" the same way but rejects it. Sometimes "man" is ambiguous because of gender, and sometimes because of species.

The key Chinese term here, *ren* (人), has some ambiguity, though not about gender. It can mean "human" or it can mean "person," - Pippin is a person but not a human. Deng's translation reads: "His name is Peregrin, [he] is an extremely valiant *ren*." Ingold: "*Ren*?" Pippin: "*Ren*! Am not! I am a hobbit *ren* (a hobbit person)" (Deng, *RK*, 7). This keeps the ambiguity but adds the complication that to be a hobbit is also to be a hobbit-*ren*. It goes back and forth: a brave person-*ren*; a human-*ren*? No, a hobbit *person*-ren. Zhu makes it explicit: "He is called Peregrin, [he] is an extremely brave *ren*." "*Ren*?" says Ingold, but then Pippin says, "*Renlei*! (human being) [...] *renlei*! Am not! I am a hobbit *ren*" (Zhu, *RK*, 22).

The muddle of Pippin's classification as it moves into Chinese might be no more than a slight distraction, another example of a Source Text using a single word which must be translated into different words in the Target Language, depending on context. There are many similar cases, such as when Éomer is having trouble adjusting to the presence of elves and dwarves. In such a strange world, "How shall a man judge what to do in such times?" (*TT*, 'The Riders of Rohan', 427). He probably just means "how can I know what to do?" He is not implying women have a better answer to his puzzlement. Yet, so soon after he has mused on elves and dwarves, surely it also means, "how can human beings know?" Deng uses the gender-neutral *ren*: "how should a human/person judge for himself what to do?" (Deng, *TT*, 37). Yilin avoids the pronoun: "These years it is hard to say what to do?" (Yilin, *TT*, 35). But Zhu accents Éomer's self-identification as not-marvellous, and also gendered male: "How can a common man (*fanfu suzi* 凡夫俗子, common-male common-son) under these circumstances, make a true judgement?" (Zhu, *TT*, 54).

But there is one place where this problem is crucial to the story itself. Éowyn falls in love with Aragorn but is gently rebuffed, and she begins to actively seek her own death in battle. She dresses up as a man, and takes a man's name. Like Queen Elizabeth she claims "the heart of a man," along the way taking pity on Merry who has likewise been excluded from military service. Finally they plunge into the Battle of Pelennor Fields. King Théoden is mortally wounded and lies unprotected. When the monstrous Witch-King approaches to finish him off, Éowyn confronts the enemy:

> [Éowyn:] 'Do what you will; but I will hinder it, if I may.'
> 'Hinder me? Thou fool. No living man may hinder me!'
> […] 'But no living man am I! You look upon a woman'
> (*RK*, 'The Battle of the Pelennor Fields', 823)

Why is the Witch-King so very confident he can't be killed? Long before, Glorfindel made a prophecy. The Witch-King was fleeing a defeat, and Glorfindel told others not to pursue him. "Far off yet is his doom, and not by the hand of man will he fall" (*RK*, Appendix A, I, iv). Note: small-m "man," not "a man" or capital-M "Man." Here we have the ungrammatical small-m "man," which we might blame on the transcription of Glorfindel's utterance - after all, we can't actually *hear* upper and lower cases. Tolkien wanted to leave it ambiguous, and so he seems careless here. Glorfindel's words are buried away in an appendix, but Gandalf repeats it in the story itself: "not by the hand of man shall he fall" (*RK*, 'The Siege of Gondor', 801).

The problem is that when the Witch-King says 'no living man may hinder me,' he thinks (and we think) it means 'no one' or possibly 'no human being,' but when Éowyn says, 'no living man am I,' she is saying, 'I'm alive and I'm human, but I'm not male, I'm female.' As if no one had ever imagined a woman might stab him. So the original contains a kind of verbal trick or riddle. Tolkien plays bait and switch, so as to obscure the possibility that Éowyn might kill the Witch-King. And, so as to heighten the sense of danger to Éowyn - he's going up against someone no-one can kill - but as it turns out, Glorfindel must have just meant *male*.

Éowyn's femininity functions as a kind of magic here; a

kind of partial immunity. Her helm comes off and "her bright hair, released from its bonds, gleamed with pale gold upon her shoulders" (*RK*, 'The Battle of the Pelennor Fields', 823).[1]

When the Witch-King seems about to kill her, Merry gets a stab in. Again, as the bad guy said (while being loose about the capital M), no 'man' can stop me - Merry is not a "Man" but a Hobbit, as Pippin vigorously insisted earlier - a difference of species, not gender. Between them they kill him: a Man who's not a man, and a man who's not a Man. If we take Glorfindel's words to mean male persons, it's technically true since the Witch-King is hindered but not killed by Merry; if we take it to mean human beings, it's not true. Perhaps also, since the Hobbits are frequently referred to as "halflings," "only children to your eyes" as Aragorn remarks, Merry is not fully a "man" in another sense: not yet an adult (*TT*, 'The Riders of Rohan', 424).

How do the translations handle this? In the Yilin edition, this volume was translated by Tang Dingjiu. The key moment of dialogue is:

> 'In the world there is not that person (*meiyou neige ren* 没有那个人) able to stop me!'
> […] 'Then just wait for me to deal with (*shoushi* 收拾, put in order, settle up) you!' (Yilin, *RK*, 118)

So the Yilin edition has: no person or human being (*ren*) can stop me - not gender-specific, but also only loosely species-specific, since he does not quite say no *human* (*renlei*) can kill me. But Éowyn's reply ignores the issue. She just says, wait til I deal with you! No one can stop me / I'll give it a try. Yilin's version of Glorfindel's prophecy has: "the hand of ordinary

1. On the power of her unbound hair, see Colvin 2020, 135-6.

people (*fanren de shou* 凡人的手) cannot seize him" (Yilin, *RK*, 381). It's not much of a prophecy: under the circumstances, it sounds like a bit of a put-down: let him go, it'll take more than you ordinary people to catch him. For Gandalf's repetition of the line, Tang is not much better: "other people (*bieren*) cannot strike him dead (*da busi ta*)" (Yilin, *RK*, 91).

But the translation by Zhu Xueheng does a better job:

> 'All the world's masculine heroes (*yingxiong haohan* 英雄 好漢) have no way to stop me!'
> […] 'I am not some kind of (*bushi shenme* 不是 什麽) masculine hero! Before your eyes is a woman' (Zhu, *RK*, 160).

The phrase *yingxiong haohan* is strongly masculine. *Han* has the sense of maleness, as in *laohan* 老漢 (old man) and *dahan* 大漢 (big man). *Ying* means hero, not particularly gendered; *xiong* means male, virile, as used in combinations for male animals, in medical terms such as testosterone and words starting with andro-. "Maleness" itself is *xiongxing* 雄性, male nature. So Zhu gets the gender issue: "no masculine hero can stop me / I'm not one of those masculine heroes, I'm a woman." But Zhu cannot capture the shift from man-as-person to man-as-male. It's not as if the Witch-King fears some cowardly back-stabber might do him in. Zhu's translation of Glorfindel's prophecy also uses *yingxiong haohan*, and Glorfindel's words remain a somewhat accurate prophecy because Éowyn is not male, though Éowyn becomes one of the greatest heroes of the whole story (Zhu, *RK*, Appendix, 28).

Even the talented Deng Jiawan cannot solve this puzzle. Deng's version of Glorfindel's remark is: "he cannot die by a person's (or a human's) hand (*renshou* 人手)" (Deng, *RK*, 93, 395) Here Glorfindel is simply incorrect. Then:

> 'There is no living person (*huoren* 活人) that can stop me!' […] 'But I am not a living male person (*huozhe de nanren* 活着 的 男人)! What you face is a female person (*nüren* 女人)' (Deng, *RK*, 121)

The Witch-King says no one alive can kill me, and Éowyn says I'm not alive-and-male. So Deng is fully aware of the problem and resolves the issue in two ways, by slipping in "male," and by inserting a footnote on the phrase *huoren* ("living person"): "*Huoren* (living person) can also be translated as 'living male person' (Deng, *RK*, 121). Here it has two connotations. However, her assertion here is somewhat ad hoc - there is nothing inherently gendered about *huoren*. She also footnotes the passage in the Appendixes on Éowyn's title, "Lady of the Shield-arm": "what Glorfindel said to King Eärnur a long time ago came true: the Witch-King could not die by a person's hand (*renshou*) (In English 'man' can be translated as 'humankind (*renlei*)', and also can be translated as 'male person (*nanren*)')" (Deng, *RK*, 423). Even though a footnote may not be "always a sign of weakness on the part of a translator", it registers as an interruption (Eco 2001, 50). At first sight these seem to be cases of failure or loss - none of the three translators can catch the trick.

A defeatist, zero-sum view of translations reduces retellings to lesser "versions" of the "same" story. Though Tolkien doubted translation of his work without his own involvement, 'On Fairy-stories' strongly supports the integrity of variant retellings - which must surely include translations. Following the broad consensus in Translation Studies, translations are stories in themselves. From one point of view, with the original text and three translations, we still have only one story; from another perspective, we have four - so far. While there is an obvious relation between the original text and the various translations, they are not “the same story.” Even the most “faithful” translation is to be considered “as iteration, as repetition-with-a-difference, a mode of textual proliferation rather than a mode by which semantic content is transferred” (Emmerich 2017, 161).

So pretend now that the first time you are reading this is in the Chinese - or even, imagine that Tolkien wrote it in Chinese. The Yilin edition ignores the gender aspect and emphasizes Éowyn’s suicidal fury, because she shows no sign of any hope: ‘I am invincible! / I don’t care.’ Éowyn had been seeking her own glorious death at least since Aragorn rejected her. This is surely the Northern Theory of Courage - not Éowyn cottoning on to the trick with a glimmer of hope, but persisting in the face of apparently inevitable failure. Zhu catches the gendered aspect, but also features Éowyn’s denial that she is a hero - this, after her previous protestations about not being allowed to fight in the war, and her angry assertions of her own martial skills (*RK*, ‘The Passing of the Grey Company’, 767). Zhu’s translation hints that she might be wising up a little - and indeed, after she has recovered, she moves into a traditional romantic relationship with Faramir, and they live happily ever after. It also implies she has no hope: if all these great macho heroes can’t kill you, what chance do I have? Yet I will try. Deng’s version blurs the question with a non sequitur insertion into Éowyn’s reply of the adjective “male”; but she also seems to deny that she is alive - perhaps showing her full embrace of the inevitability of her death. By the very inability to reproduce the trick of Man/man, the Chinese versions are forced to depict Éowyn as even more despairing and therefore even braver than in the original.

Bibliography

Bronowski, Jacob, *The Ascent of Man*, (BBC and Time-Life Films, 1973).

Colvin, Kathryn, "'Her Enchanted Hair': Rossetti, 'Lady Lilith,' and the Victorian Fascination with Hair as Influences on Tolkien", *Mythlore*, 39.1 (2020), 133-148.

Eco, Umberto, *Experiences in Translation*, trans. Alastair McEwen, (University of Toronto Press, 2001).

Emmerich, Karen, *Literary Translation and the Making of Originals,* (Bloomsbury, 2017).

Smith, Huston, *The Religions of Man*, (Harper and Brothers, 1958).
—, *The World's Religions*, (HarperOne, 1991).

The Lord of the Rings in Chinese

The Yilin Press translations (Nanjing, 2001) :

Mojie zaixian ('The Magic Ring Re-appears'), trans. Ding Di.
Shuangta qibing ('The Surprise Attack of the Twin Towers'), trans. Yao Jinrong.
Wangzhe wudi ('The King Is Triumphant'), trans. Yang Dingjiu.

The Zhu Xueheng translations (Linking, 2001):

Mojie xianshen ('The Magic Ring Appears').
Shuangcheng qimou ('The Ingenious Plan of the Twin Walled-Cities').
Wangzhe zailin ('The King Again Approaches').

The Deng Jiawan translations (Wenjing, 2013):

Mojie tongmeng ('Alliance/Fellowship of the magic ring').
Shuangta shutu ('Twin towers different routes').
Wangzhe Huilai ('The King Returns').

"*Las*" Silmarils or "*Los*" Silmarils? Approaches to a new Spanish translation of *The Silmarillion*

Helena Real

The Silmarillion (1977) is the seminal work by J.R.R. Tolkien when it comes to the Elder Days of Middle-earth. Although it is not without its faults - recognized by its own editor, Christopher Tolkien, in both the introduction to the original text and in others of his father's posthumous works that he edited - it still remains a fundamental read when introducing new readers to Middle-earth's earliest stories, as well as providing the most complete and coherent version of the main events that occurred during the first Three Ages of the World, before what was presented in both *The Hobbit* (1937) and *The Lord of the Rings* (1954-1955).

In Spanish, there is only one translation of *The Silmarillion*. This translation (Rubén Masera and Luis Domènech, 1984) has never been revised or widely criticized by Spanish-speaking Tolkien scholars.

In spite of what it may seem, considering these facts, the truth is that the Spanish text of *The Silmarillion* is not perfect; indeed, it has a plethora of issues. This paper will take a look at some of the most problematic of these issues, explaining why they are problematic, as well as analyzing potential alternatives on how to solve them.

As such, a new Spanish translation of *The Silmarillion* seems not only a worthy endeavor, but something sorely needed in order to present readers with a translation that is as accurate and faithful to Tolkien's original text as possible.

1 - The Problem of Gender

The first, and perhaps most self-evident of the issues in *The Silmarillion*'s Spanish translation is that of the name of the jewels at the center of the narrative: the Silmarils or *Silmarilli* in Quenya.

Nouns in Spanish are gendered as either masculine or feminine. Because of that, when translating a phrase such as "the Silmarils" into Spanish, the translator needs to decide whether to use a masculine or feminine gender for the article.

The Spanish translators decided to go for the masculine, rendering the official translation as "*Los* Silmarils". This is most probably the result of the "rule" that the *Real Academia de la Lengua Española* or RAE (Royal Academy of the Spanish Language) has, which states that the masculine gender is the default and/or neutral (*Diccionario panhispánico de dudas*, 2005). So, in case of doubt about gender - such as when translating a foreign work - the masculine is preferred.

In contrast with other languages - and as a relic of their colonialist past - the Spanish language has an institution that is dedicated to regulating what the Spanish language is supposed to be. Following an outdated prescriptive approach to linguistics, this institution - the RAE - still to this day tries to dictate what is right (and wrong) when speaking and writing in Spanish. Needless to say, the RAE has come under a lot of criticism in recent times for their decisions, especially when it comes to denying recognition to the rise of alternatives to represent a true neutral gender in Spanish.

Going back to the translation of "the Silmarils" as "*Los* Silmarils", this decision is at least questionable from the in-fiction perspective. The Silmarils are usually referred to by Tolkien as "the Great Jewels", which in Spanish would translate as "*Las Grandes Joyas*". Moreover, the conflict between the Noldor and Morgoth (and the Oath of Fëanor and the subsequent Doom of Mandos, of course) is later referred to as "The War of the Jewels" which, in Spanish, would be (and has been) translated as "*La Guerra de las Joyas*".

Spanish speakers know that the translation of "jewel" is "*joya*", which is a feminine noun. Considering that the rule in Spanish is that both article and noun must have the same number and gender (*Diccionario panhispánico de dudas*, 2005), the correct translation of "the Silmarils" into Spanish, then, should be "*Las* Silmarils", because "Silmaril" is here functioning as *joya*, a feminine noun.

This is an emblematic example of a recurring problem in the 1984 Spanish translation of *The Silmarillion*: a lack of understanding and/or consideration by the translators of Tolkien's work. They don't seem to know - or care - why Tolkien chose certain words and or ways of expression and, what's worse, make no effort to incorporate those choices into their translation.

Let us examine some further examples.

2 - "Ere" is not the same as "Before"

The writing style of *The Silmarillion* is one of its most distinguishing characteristics. It has often been compared to that of King James's version of *The Bible* (1611) (Hensler, 2013), because of the use of archaisms and manners of speech that are not common in Modern English.

As an example: Tolkien uses (and abuses) the word "ere" in the text, almost never opting for the more common alternative "before". This is so obvious and repetitive that it is not something that can easily be ignored, but something that a translator would have to address as one of their first translation decisions to make.

Here is a telling example from the very beginning of the *Quenta Silmarillion*,

> It is told among the wise that the First War began *before* Arda was full-shaped, and *ere* yet there was anything that grew or walked upon earth. (1977, 35; emphasis mine)

In the Spanish translation, it reads,

> Se dice entre los sabios que la Primera Guerra estalló *antes* de que Arda estuviera del todo acabada, *y antes* de que nada creciera o anduviera sobre la Tierra. (1984, 35; emphasis mine)

Regrettably, the Spanish translation ignores the difficulty and original stylistic decision and simply translates "ere" as "*antes*", a very common word in Spanish that is most often used to translate "before" - even in the same sentence.

Now, the Spanish language has plenty of synonyms and even archaisms of its own to translate "ere" as something other than "before"; for example, the word "*denante*", which is a rarely used adverb in Spanish could work here perfectly to translate the original archaism. The only reasons that would justify using "*antes*" would be a) that the translators don't know and/or understand the use of the word "ere" by Tolkien or b) that they have purposefully ignored the writer's word choice. As you will see later on - with another issue - there is enough textual evidence to believe, I think, that it is most probably this latter option than the former that explains this unbelievable oversight.

Be that as it may, in ignoring Tolkien's stylistic word choice, Masera and Domènech made *The Silmarillion* translation into Spanish all the poorer.

3 - The Loss of Formal Addressing

Another example where the translators have overlooked Tolkien's style is when characters are formally addressing one another. This appears often throughout the texts that make up *The Silmarillion*, but it is never clearer than on *Ainulindalë*, the book's first section.

Ainulindalë is a text that is reminiscent in style and content to *The Bible*'s "Genesis" section. Because of that, it should surprise nobody that, when Tolkien chose to have Eru Ilúvatar (god) speak with the Ainur (archangels), he chose to employ the now archaic, Early Modern English second-person singular and plural pronouns, exemplified by "thee", "thou", and "ye" and their corresponding verbal conjugations.

Whereas we see Tolkien use these terms in *Ainulindalë*:

> Then Ilúvatar spoke, and he said: 'Mighty are the Ainur, and mightiest among them is Melkor; but that he may know, and all the Ainur, that I am Ilúvatar, those things that ye have sung, I will show them forth, that ye may see what ye have done. And *thou*, Melkor, shalt see that no theme may be played that hath not its uttermost source in me, nor can any alter the music in my despite. For he that attempteth this shall prove but mine instrument in the devising of things more wonderful, which he himself hath not imagined.' (1977, 17; emphasis mine)

The Spanish translation, in contrast, uses the common forms for second-person pronouns.

> Entonces Ilúvatar habló, y dijo: - Poderosos son los Ainur, y entre ellos el más poderoso es Melkor; pero sepan él y todos los Ainur que yo soy Ilúvatar; *os* mostraré las cosas que habéis cantado y así *veréis* qué *habéis* hecho. Y *tú*, Melkor, verás que ningún tema puede tocarse que no tenga en mí su fuente más profunda, y que nadie puede alterar la música a mi pesar. Porque aquel que lo intente probará que es sólo mi instrumento para la creación de cosas más maravillosas todavía, que él no ha imaginado. (1984, 13-4; emphasis mine)

In the first three instances, the translators implied the use of the form "*vos*", which is the equivalent of "thou", "thee", and "ye" in Spanish. The problem is that these formal forms are now common in Spanish spoken in Spain, so Spanish-speaking readers cannot discern a difference between the way Ilúvatar speaks and any other character in *The Silmarillion*.

In this case, I consider that a great solution would be to translate all the text into Neutral Spanish - i.e., a Spanish that uses "*tú*" and "*ustedes*" (and derived forms) for the second-person pronouns singular and plural, respectively - and save these forms, "*vos*", and "*vosotros*", which are archaic and in disuse in all Spanish-speaking countries that are not Spain (the immense majority), for these instances in which Tolkien employs the archaic forms for stylistic reasons.

The last archaic form in the paragraph, "thou", is grossly mistranslated by Masera and Domènech by using "*tú*", which is the most common form of second-person pronoun in Spanish. This totally ruins the style of the paragraph and makes it so Ilúvatar speaks formally to all the Ainur, but disrespects Melkor or treats him especially warmly, which is most emphatically not Tolkien's intention in the original.

This is probably the best example of how an obvious mistake changes the meaning/tone of the original.

Still, there is another more disturbing tendency in Masera and Domènech's translation of *The Silmarillion*: that of adding text to the translation that wasn't there in the original.

4 - Introducing New Text

All the translation issues discussed above can be explained as either oversight or decisions. But the deliberate choice to add text during the translation process borders on unethical.

Whereas Tolkien writes:

> There was Eru, the One, who in Arda is called Ilúvatar; and he made first the Ainur, the Holy Ones, that were the offspring of his thought, and they were with him before aught else was made. (1977, 15)

The Spanish translation reads as:

> *En el principio* estaba Eru, el Único, que en Arda es llamado Ilúvatar; y primero hizo a los Ainur, los Sagrados, que eran vástagos de su pensamiento, y estuvieron con él antes que se hiciera alguna otra cosa. (1984, 11; emphasis mine)

The beginning of the Spanish translation introduces a phrase that isn't there in Tolkien's text: "*En el principio*", which means "In the beginning" in English. There's no explanation or reason why Masera and Domènech stated anywhere that could at least explain - if not excuse - the translators introducing material in their translation that was most emphatically not there in the original.

The only reason imaginable why they did this is to imitate *The Bible*'s "Genesis" section which begins, at least in the

Spanish version, with the same words: "*En el principio.*" Even if they did so because they were trying to emphasize the connection between *Ainulindalë* and "Genesis", nothing justifies this unwarranted intrusion and, dare I say, lack of work ethics.

The implications of such a way of translating a work of art are, to say, disturbing, as it really puts all the translation effort into question. Translations of works of art are, by default, messy affairs. In translating a work of art, the translator(s) are trying to create not only something that is legible, but something that resembles the original in meaning and style so that, in doing so, they are creating what amounts to a new work of art. It may very well be impossible to create the perfect translation - the one that actually is a work of art as similar as possible to the original - but, when easy mistakes are made (either because of laziness or ignorance) and the work ethics of those involved leaves as much to be desired, as it is in this case, the task proves not only impossible but seemingly futile.

5 - Conclusions

Is it possible to trust that the work Masera and Domènech did produced an accurate and reliable translation of *The Silmarillion* into Spanish, one that actually presents the readers with something that reflects Tolkien's ideas and style when writing the original? It is the opinion of this writer that they didn't. *The Silmarillion* Spanish speakers have is, in my assessment, one that may produce in the readers a wrong impression of what Tolkien was actually trying to say, thanks to the faulty work the translators did.

Because of this, it is my evaluation that this translation, perpetrated by Masera and Domènech in 1984 - and that has never been revised or edited - is a text that must be retired and replaced by a new version as soon as possible. It is my hope that a new translation could not only solve the problems hereby presented, but also improve the general style of the text.

Although some could argue that if such a translation followed some of my preferences - such as translating English archaisms for Spanish archaisms - could create a text that is less accessible, I would argue that doing so would be in the spirit of remaining faithful to the original.

Moreover, I would go as far as to say that it is better to have a more challenging but respectful text than an easier to read one. This is so because, in essence, an easier-to-read text is in reality a simplified version of the original, which loses many (if not all) of the intricacies the author originally intended.

Bibliography

Hensler, Kevin R. "God and Ilúvatar: Tolkien's Use of Biblical Parallels and Tropes in His Cosmogony" (Proceedings of the 2nd Mythgard Institute Mythmoot, 2013).

Tolkien, J.R.R., *The Silmarillion*, (London: George Allen & Unwin, 1977).
— *El Silmarillion*, translated by Rubén Masera and Luis Domènech (Capellades:
Ediciones Minotauro, 1984).

Las Silmarils o *Los* Silmarils? Aproximaciones a una nueva traducción al español de *El Silmarillion*

Helena Real

El Silmarillion (1977) es el trabajo seminal de J.R.R. Tolkien cuando se trata de los Días Antiguos de la Tierra Media. Aunque no está exento de defectos - reconocidos por su propio editor, Christopher Tolkien, tanto en la introducción al texto original como en otras de las obras póstumas de su padre que editó - sigue siendo una lectura fundamental a la hora de introducir a les nueves lectores a las primeras historias de la Tierra Media, además de brindar la versión más completa y coherente de los principales acontecimientos ocurridos durante las primeras Tres Edades del Mundo, antes de lo presentado en tanto *El Hobbit* (1937) como *El Señor de los Anillos* (1954-1955).

En español, sólo existe una traducción de tan importante texto en la obra de Tolkien. Esta traducción - de Rubén Masera y Luis Domènech, de 1984 - nunca ha sido revisada ni criticada ampliamente por les estudioses de Tolkien de habla hispana.

A pesar de lo que pueda parecer, a la vista de estos hechos, lo cierto es que el texto en español de *El Silmarillion* no es perfecto; de hecho, tiene una plétora de problemas. Este artículo analizará algunos de sus aspectos más problemáticos, explicará por qué lo son y analizará posibles alternativas sobre cómo resolverlos.

Como tal, una nueva traducción al español de *El Silmarillion* parece no sólo un esfuerzo digno, sino algo muy necesario para presentar a les lectores una traducción que sea lo más precisa y fiel posible al texto original de Tolkien.

1 - El problema del género

El primero, y quizás el más evidente de los problemas en la traducción al español de *El Silmarillion* es el nombre de las joyas en el centro de la narrativa: los silmarils o *silmarilli* en Quenya.

Los sustantivos en español siempre tienen un género, masculino o femenino. Por eso, al traducir una frase como «*the Silmarills*» al español, le traductore debe decidir si usará género masculino o femenino para el artículo correspondiente.

Los traductores españoles decidieron optar por el masculino, resultando en la traducción oficial como «los Silmarils». Este es muy probablemente el resultado de la «regla» de la Real Academia de la Lengua Española o RAE, que establece que el género masculino es el predeterminado y/o neutro (*Diccionario panhispánico de dudas*, 2005). Entonces, en caso de duda sobre el género, como cuando se traduce una obra extranjera, se prefiere el masculino.

A diferencia de otros idiomas, y como una reliquia de su pasado colonial, el idioma español tiene una institución que se dedica a regular lo que se supone es el idioma español. Siguiendo un enfoque prescriptivo obsoleto acerca de la lingüística, esta institución, la RAE, aún hoy trata de dictar lo que está bien (y lo que está mal) al hablar y escribir en español. Ni que decir que la RAE ha sido objeto de muchas críticas en los últimos tiempos por sus decisiones, especialmente cuando se trata de negar reconocimiento al auge de alternativas para representar un verdadero género neutro en español.

Volviendo a la traducción de «*the Silmarils*» como «los Silmarils», esta decisión es al menos cuestionable desde la perspectiva de la ficción. Tolkien suele referirse a los Silmarils como «*the Great Jewels*», que en español se traduciría como «las Grandes Joyas». Además, el conflicto entre les Noldor y Morgoth (y el Juramento de Fëanor y la subsiguiente Maldición de Mandos, por supuesto) se denomina más tarde «*The War of the Jewels*», que en español sería (y ha sido) traducido como «La Guerra de las Joyas».

Les hispanohablantes sabemos que la traducción de «*jewel*» es «joya», que es un sustantivo femenino. Considerando que la regla en español es que tanto el artículo como el sustantivo deben tener el mismo número y género (*Diccionario panhispánico de dudas*, 2005), la traducción correcta de «*the Silmarils*» al español, entonces, debería ser «las Silmarils», porque «Silmaril» aquí funciona como «joya», un sustantivo femenino.

Este es un ejemplo emblemático de un problema recurrente en la traducción al español de 1984 de *El Silmarillion*: falta de comprensión y/o consideración por parte de los traductores de la obra de Tolkien. No parecen saber, ni preocuparse, por qué Tolkien eligió ciertas palabras o formas de expresión y, lo que es peor, no hacen ningún esfuerzo por incorporar esas elecciones en su traducción.

Examinemos algunos ejemplos más.

2 - «*Ere*» no es lo mismo que «*before*»

El estilo de escritura de *El Silmarillion* es una de sus características más distintivas. A menudo se ha comparado con la versión de King James de *La Biblia* (1611) (Hensler, 2013), debido al uso de arcaísmos y formas de hablar que no son comunes en el inglés moderno.

Como ejemplo: Tolkien usa (y abusa) de la palabra «ere» en el texto, optando casi nunca por la alternativa más común «*before*». Esto es tan obvio y repetitivo que no es algo que pueda ignorarse fácilmente, sino algo que une traductore tendría que abordar como una de sus primeras decisiones de traducción.

Aquí hay un ejemplo revelador desde el comienzo mismo del *Quenta Silmarillion*,

> It is told among the wise that the First War began *before* Arda was full-shaped, and *ere* yet there was anything that grew or walked upon earth. (1977, 35; mi negrita)

En la traducción al español, se lee,

> Se dice entre los sabios que la Primera Guerra estalló *antes* de que Arda estuviera del todo acabada, y *antes* de que nada creciera o anduviera sobre la Tierra. (1984, 35; mi negrita)

Lamentablemente, la traducción al español ignora la dificultad y la decisión estilística original y simplemente traduce «*ere*» como «antes», una palabra muy común en español que se usa con mayor frecuencia para traducir «*before*», incluso en la misma oración.

Ahora bien, al idioma español le sobran sinónimos y hasta arcaísmos propios para traducir «*ere*» como algo distinto a «antes»; por ejemplo, la palabra «denante», que es un adverbio poco utilizado en español, podría funcionar aquí perfectamente para traducir el arcaísmo original. Las únicas razones que justificarían el uso de «antes» serían a) que los traductores no conocen y/o no entienden el uso de la palabra «*ere*» por parte de Tolkien o b) que han ignorado deliberadamente la elección de palabras del escritor. Como se verá más adelante, con otro problema, hay suficiente evidencia textual para creer, en mi parecer, que es más probable que esta última opción que la primera explique a este increíble descuido.

Sea como fuere, al ignorar la elección de palabras estilísticas de Tolkien, Masera y Domènech hicieron *El Silmarillion* traducción al español cuanto más pobre estilísticamente.

3 - La pérdida de la formalidad al dirigirse

Otro ejemplo en el que los traductores han pasado por alto el estilo de Tolkien es cuando los personajes se dirigen formalmente entre sí. Esto aparece a menudo a lo largo de los textos que componen *El Silmarillion*, pero nunca es más claro que en *Ainulindalë*, la primera sección del libro.

Ainulindalë es un texto que recuerda en estilo y contenido a la sección del "Génesis" de *La Biblia*. Por eso, no debería sorprender a nadie que, cuando Tolkien eligió que Eru Ilúvatar (dios) hablara con les Ainur (arcángeles), optó por emplear los ahora arcaicos pronombres de segunda persona del singular y del plural del inglés moderno temprano, ejemplificados por «*thee*», «*thou*», y «*ye*» y sus correspondientes conjugaciones verbales.

Mientras que vemos a Tolkien usar estos términos en *Ainulindale*:

> Then Ilúvatar spoke, and he said: 'Mighty are the Ainur, and mightiest among them is Melkor; but that he may know, and all the Ainur, that I am Ilúvatar, those things that ye have sung, I will show them forth, that ye may see what ye have done. And *thou*, Melkor, shalt see that no theme may be played that hath not its uttermost source in me, nor can any alter the music in my despite. For he that attempteth this shall prove but mine instrument in the devising of things more wonderful, which he himself hath not imagined.' (1977, 17; mi negrita)

La traducción al español, en cambio, usa las formas comunes para los pronombres de segunda persona.

> Entonces Ilúvatar habló, y dijo: - Poderosos son los Ainur, y entre ellos el más poderoso es Melkor; pero sepan él y todos los Ainur que yo soy Ilúvatar; *os* mostraré las cosas que habéis cantado y así *veréis* qué *habéis* hecho. Y *tú*, Melkor, verás que ningún tema puede tocarse que no tenga en mí su fuente más profunda, y que nadie puede alterar la música a mi pesar. Porque aquel que lo intente probará que es sólo mi instrumento para la creación de cosas más maravillosas todavía, que él no ha imaginado. (1984, 13-4; mi negrita)

En los primeros tres casos, los traductores dieron a entender el uso de la forma «vos», que es el equivalente de «*thou*», «*thee*» y «*ye*» en español. El problema es que estas formas formales ahora son comunes en el español que se habla en España, por lo que les lectores de habla hispana no pueden discernir una diferencia entre la forma en que habla Ilúvatar y cualquiere otre personaje en *El Silmarillion*.

En este caso, considero que una gran solución sería traducir todo el texto en español neutro - es decir, un español que usa «tú» y «ustedes» (y formas derivadas) para los pronombres de segunda persona singular y plural, respectivamente - y guarde estas formas, «vos», y «vosotros», las cuales son arcaicas y en desuso en todos los países de habla hispana que no son España (la inmensa mayoría), por estos casos en los que Tolkien emplea las formas arcaicas por razones estilísticas.

La última forma arcaica del párrafo, «*thou*», está muy mal traducida por Masera y Domènech al usar «tú», que es la forma más común de pronombre de segunda persona en español. Esto arruina totalmente el estilo del párrafo y hace que Ilúvatar le hable formalmente a todes les Ainur, pero le falte el respeto a Melkor o lo trate con especial calidez, lo que enfáticamente no es la intención de Tolkien en el original.

Este es probablemente el mejor ejemplo de cómo un error obvio cambia el significado/tono del original.

Aún así, hay otra tendencia más inquietante en la traducción de Masera y Domènech de *El Silmarillio*n: la de añadir texto a la traducción que no estaba en el original.

4 - Introducción de texto nuevo

Todos los problemas de traducción discutidos anteriormente pueden explicarse como descuidos o decisiones. Pero la elección deliberada de agregar texto durante el proceso de traducción raya en la falta de ética.

Mientras que Tolkien escribe:

> There was Eru, the One, who in Arda is called Ilúvatar; and he made first the Ainur, the Holy Ones, that were the offspring of his thought, and they were with him before aught else was made. (1977, 15)

La traducción al español dice así:

> *En el principio* estaba Eru, el Único, que en Arda es llamado Ilúvatar; y primero hizo a los Ainur, los Sagrados, que eran vástagos de su pensamiento, y estuvieron con él antes que se hiciera alguna otra cosa. (1984, 11; mi negrita)

La traducción al español comienza introduciendo una frase que no está en el texto de Tolkien: «En el principio». No hay ninguna explicación o razón que Masera y Domènech hayan mencionado algo que al menos pudiera explicar, si no excusar, que los traductores introdujeran material en su traducción que, de manera muy enfática, no estaba en el original.

La única razón imaginable por la que hicieron esto es para imitar la sección del "Génesis" de *La Biblia*, la que comienza, al menos en la versión en español, con las mismas palabras: «En el principio». Incluso si lo hicieron porque estaban tratando de enfatizar la conexión entre *Ainulindalë* y el "Génesis", nada justifica esta intromisión injustificada y, me atrevo a decir, falta de ética laboral.

Las implicaciones de tal forma de traducir una obra de arte son, por decir lo menos, inquietantes, ya que realmente ponen en tela de juicio todo el esfuerzo de traducción. Las traducciones de obras de arte son, por defecto, asuntos complicados. Al traducir una obra de arte, les traductores están tratando de crear no sólo algo que sea legible, sino algo que se asemeje al original en significado y estilo para que, al hacerlo, creen lo que equivale a una nueva obra de arte. Puede ser imposible crear la traducción perfecta, la que en realidad es una obra de arte lo más similar posible al original, pero cuando se cometen errores fáciles (ya sea por pereza o ignorancia) y la ética de trabajo de les involucrades deja mucho que desear, como lo es en este caso, la tarea resulta no sólo imposible sino aparentemente fútil.

5 - Conclusiones

¿Es posible confiar en que el trabajo de Masera y Domènech produjo una traducción fiel y fidedigna de *El Silmarillion* al español, una que realmente presente a les lectores algo que refleje las ideas y el estilo de Tolkien al escribir el original? Es la opinión de esta escritora que no. *El Silmarillion* que tienen les hispanohablantes es, a mi juicio, uno que puede producir en les lectores una impresión equivocada de lo que Tolkien en realidad estaba tratando de decir, gracias al trabajo defectuoso de los traductores.

Por ello, es mi evaluación que esta traducción, perpetrada por Masera y Domènech en 1984 - y que nunca ha sido revisada ni editada - es un texto que debe ser retirado y reemplazado por una nueva versión lo antes posible. Tengo la esperanza de que una nueva traducción no sólo pueda resolver los problemas aquí presentados, sino también mejorar el estilo general del texto.

Aunque algunos podrían argumentar que si tal traducción siguiera algunas de mis preferencias, como traducir arcaísmos del inglés por arcaísmos del español, podría crear un texto menos accesible, yo diría que hacerlo de esta forma estaría en concordancia con el espíritu de permanecer fiel al original.

Además, me atrevería a decir que es mejor tener un texto más desafiante pero respetuoso que uno más fácil de leer. Esto es así porque, en esencia, un texto más fácil de leer es, en realidad, sólo una versión simplificada del original, que pierde muchas (sino todas) las complejidades que el autor pretendía originalmente.

Characterisation and depiction of nature in the Spanish translation of *Roverandom*

Martha Celis Mendoza
and Aline Esperanza Maza Vázquez

The different elements that involve the formation of characters in any literary work, from their names to their descriptions, and the way they express themselves, have a definite impact on the readers' reception. Also, while the plot drives the development of such works, it is by means of description that authors manage to transport their audiences into the world they are portraying. This is especially relevant in the case of science-fiction and fantasy books, where the suspension of disbelief proposed by Samuel Taylor Coleridge can take place thanks to the writers' mastery. Such responsibility lies in the hands of the translator in the case of works rendered into a foreign language. We will present some relevant examples of these categories to analyze how translators overcome those challenges in *Roverandom*.

1 - Characterization

Despite being almost contemporaneous to the creation of *The Hobbit*, *Roverandom* did not see the public light until many years later. This is perhaps one of the reasons for the relative lack of scholarly criticism and translations into other languages, as is the case with many of Tolkien's works. Another possible reason is that it only has a subtle relation to the worlds and characters belonging to the more canonical works of the legendarium, with just a few references to "Elvenhome itself and the land of Faery"

(Shippey 2008, xiv). The very brief number of scholarly works on Roverandom is not only due to its relatively short public life, merely a couple of decades from its first edition in 1998, but also because it is still considered a tale just for Tolkien's children, and is not a prominent part of the legendarium; Janet Brennan Croft mentions that "though the underlying tale shares the immram's structure of transgression (exile) penitence and reconciliation, it feels whimsical and 'miniaturized' in a way Tolkien later came to dislike, and condemned in his 1939 essay 'On Fairy-stories'" (2018, 3). However, some critics have identified significant parallels between some of the characters in the text and the most iconic ones from the larger canon. Only a handful of studies are dedicated, partially or exclusively, to aspects of this work; among them is Romuald Lakowsky's study on the dragon, Emma Hawkins's study of the presence of dogs in Tolkien's works, and Jennifer Marchant's analysis of the three Rovers as Tolkien's use of "the double" (in this case triple, or rather, a double "double," since the three Rovers don't share a space).

For Spanish translators, a few aspects present quite a challenge in the Spanish translation, such as the way nature is depicted in the book, the representation of the three Rovers, another triad: the three wizards (Artaxerxes, Psamathos, and the Man-in-the-Moon), and the three female characters (Two's mom, his grandmother, and Artaxerxes's princess wife), but that triad is clearly unbalanced in terms of characterization, so we must leave it aside in this analysis.

The title itself, being also the name of the protagonist, constitutes one of those untranslatable conundrums, particularly considering that he will be meeting two namesakes during the course of his adventures. The name Rover, as we know, was a pièce de résistance in canine onomastics.[1] However, the referent might be obscure for someone outside the English-speaking tradition. In a language forum of the well-known online dictionary Wordreference.com, we can find the consequence of a confused translator's query into this problematic quotation: "If Rover needs to relieve tension over a lost bone or a cat that got away," to which the user (a non-native speaker of English) posed the following question: "Why is the first letter of 'Rover' written in the capital letter? Does Rover mean dogs here?" A helpful member of the forum replied, "'Rover' is a very common name for a male dog and is instantly recognizable as such, so here it stands for 'someone's pet dog.' Most dogs like to 'rove' when they get the chance."[2]

One of its meanings, "wanderer," is appropriate for the far-away adventures Roverandom's protagonist must endure. This has been frequently adopted in Spanish, at least in Mexico, with a joking tone when giving a name to a stray dog that is welcomed in the household, *Solovino* ("*solo vino*," meaning "he came on his own"). Nevertheless, the problem is transforming that name when it has had a previous owner. As Jennifer Marchant explains, "The moon-dog's story is relatively brief. He explains that his name of "Rover" suited him well" "I was a Rover too'" he confesses (Marchant 2019, 25). "I never would stop anywhere or belong to anyone before I came here. I did nothing but run away from the time I was a puppy" (*Perilous Realm*, 25). Thus, the Man-in-the-Moon decides to name him Roverandom to avoid confusion. The connotation of the particle "random" cannot be explained by a periphrasis, like in the case of "Rover, el vagabundo," which

1. Rather surprisingly, the name Rover did not even appear among the top 100 dog names on the website named, ironically, rover.com.
2. https://forum.wordreference.com/threads/rover.3517351/.

doesn't pose a problem since it is only implied in the English name but never explained:

> Yo fui el primer perro que se llamó Rover, el Vagabundo, hace miles de años; por lo tanto, ¡a ti te tuvieron que poner el nombre de Rover después de mí! ¡Yo también era un vagabundo! Nunca me quedaba quieto en un sitio, ni pertenecí a nadie antes de venir aquí. Desde que era un cachorro no hice otra cosa que escaparme. (*Cuentos desde el Reino Peligroso*, 47)[3]

Later in the book, after Roverandom has become friends with the sea Rover, he asserts how he is entitled to the name Rover. By means of the sea Rover's assertion, Tolkien explains he is using one of the other meanings of the word, a sea-rover; the Spanish translation on the other hand goes on to use the word *pirata* directly:

> Creo que yo soy el primero de todos los perros que se llaman Rover. Mi primer amo fue un rover, un auténtico vagabundo, un pirata que navegaba con su barco por las aguas del norte; era un barco muy largo, con velas rojas, y en la proa llevaba tallado un dragón, lo llamaban Gusano Rojo, y me gustaba mucho. (80)[4]

3. "'I was the first dog that was ever called Rover, thousands of years ago - so you must have been called Rover after me! I *was* a Rover too! I never would stop anywhere, or belong to anyone before I came here. I did nothing but run away from the time I was a puppy.'" (*Perilous Realm*, 26-7).

4. "'I expect I'm the first of all dog Rovers. My first master was a Rover, a real one, a sea-rover who sailed his ship in the northern waters; it was a long ship with red sails, and it was carved like a dragon in the prow, and he called it the Red Worm and loved it.'" (*Perilous Realm*, 70).

The strategy of the translators of the Spanish version in terms of onomastics is consistent; where names have a semantic meaning, such as the Man-in-the-Moon, they offer the Spanish content equivalence, *el Hombre de la Luna*; in all the other cases, they decide to maintain the names almost exactly as in the English original, making just the necessary phonetic adaptations so that the names can be pronounced, as in the case of Psamathos, changing the phoneme th, with no exact Spanish equivalent, to a simple t; the PS, in the beginning, is preserved as its use, or lack thereof, contributes to the characterization of Psamathos, as we can see in this example:

> ¡De modo que has vuelto! Pensé que no tardarías en cansarte del viejo P-sámatos (y bufó para emitir una exagerada P). Él no puede hacerlo todo. Bueno, ¿a qué has venido? Estamos en una fiesta y has interrumpido la música. (77)[5]

The same is done with Artaxerxes to make it consistent with the traditional Spanish spelling of the Persian king Jerjes: "Por favor, señor Ertejerjes, quiero decir, Artajerjes - empezó a decir Rover, más bien atropelladamente y procurando ser muy educado" (77).[6] It must be noted that in the Spanish version, Rover manages to pronounce the name right on his second attempt, whereas in the original, he gets even more confused over the correct pronunciation.

5. "'So you've turned up! I thought you would get tired of old P-samathos' (how he snorted over that exaggerated P) 'before long. He can't do quite everything. Well, what have you come down here for? We are just having a party, and you're interrupting the music.'" (*Perilous Realm*, 65).
6. "'Please, Mr Arterxaxes, I mean, Ertaxarxes,' began Rover, rather flustered and trying to be very polite." (*Perilous Realm*, 65).

A complicated and maybe not so-fortunate instance is the case of the PAM; the initials must be maintained probably not for the reference to the nickname of Lord Palmerston, as mentioned by Christine Scull and Wayne C. Hammond, but also for its phonetic quality, therefore making it impossible for the translators to change it to MAP. This provokes the inconsistency of the use of "el PAM" or "PAM" when using it as a proper name or a title, but also the awkward formulation repeated twice in the book, "en el Pacífico y el Atlántico como Mago" (77). "Estaba bastante abrumado por su propia importancia (con extranjeros), desde su matrimonio con la hija del rico rey de los mares, y su destino en el Pacífico y el Atlántico como Mago (la gente lo llamaba en forma abreviada PAM, cuando no estaba delante)" (*Cuentos desde el Reino Peligroso*, 77).[7] While Artaxerxes's description might remind us of Tom Bombadil, his wife's (also known as *Princesa Pam*) might also echo in our ears as that of Goldberry. On the other hand, when considering the use of elevated language, as mentioned in Scull and Hammond's introduction, one must take into consideration Tolkien's assertion in one of his letters: "'A good vocabulary,' he once wrote (April 1959), 'is not acquired by reading books written according to some notion of the vocabulary of one's age-group. It comes from reading books above one'" (Scull and Hammond 1998, 24). We can see one example here with the word "monsergas", and the word "galimatías" in the following fragments, both corresponding to the original "rigmaroles": "Venga la explicación, y que sea

7. "He had become rather full of his own importance (with strangers), since his marriage to the rich mer-king's daughter, and his appointment to the post of Pacific and Atlantic Magician (the PAM, they called him for short, when he was not present)." (*Perilous Realm*, 65-6).

corta; no tengo tiempo para largos galimatías" (*Cuentos desde el Reino Peligroso*, 77).[8]

> En este momento, Artajerjes estaba sentado a su lado, y tuviera o no tuviera tiempo para largas monsergas, estaba escuchando la de su esposa. O la había estado escuchando antes de que apareciera Rover. La señora Artajerjes puso fin a su monserga y a su costura, tan pronto como vio a Rover, y tras deslizarse hacia abajo lo capturó y lo llevó al asiento. (78)[9]

The Spanish version even supplies two different high-register terms for a single one in the original, perhaps with the intention of avoiding the homogenisation deformative trend, identified by Antoine Berman by overcompensating, introducing a wider variety of terms: "*Elle consiste a unifier sur tous les plans le tissu de l'original, alors que celui-ci est originairement hétérogène [...] un tendance en soi, qui plonge profondément ses racines dans l'être du traducteur*" (Berman 95, 60).[10] It is an acknowledged fact that one of the goals of children's literature is language acquisition and semantic expansion, and in this, *Roverandom* excels.

8. "'Get on to the explanation, and make it short; I've no time for long rigmaroles.'" (*Perilous Realm*, 65).
9. "Artaxerxes was at the moment sitting beside her, and whether he had the time or not for long rigmaroles, he was listening to one of her wife's- Or had been, before Rover turned up. Mrs Artaxerxes put an end to her rigmarole, and to her sockmending, as soon as she caught sight of him, and floating down picked him up and carried him back to her couch." (*Perilous Realm*, 67).
10. "It consists in unifying all the planes of the fabric of the original, whereas it is originally heterogeneous. [...] a tendency in itself, deeply rooted in the being of the translator" (translation is my own).

2 - Depiction of Nature

Scull and Hammond's notes for the first *Roverandom* edition are fundamental to understanding the story's wordplay.[11] Unfortunately, the version that appears in *Tales from the Perilous Realm* does not have them, and if in English, this could cause some trouble; in the Spanish translation, many things are lost because they do not make sense.

The first example we will mention is the wordplay Tolkien makes with the sounds and descriptions of the flowers in the second chapter. Tolkien makes a simile using names and musical instruments, which does not appear in the Spanish translation, and is even cut short by taking advantage of Tolkien's words: "and many others with untranslatable names":

> Los ruidos que había, venían sobre todo de las plantas. Las flores - las campanas blancas, las campanas claras y las campanas de plata, las campanas tintineantes y las trompetitas y los cuernos de crema (una crema muy pálida) y muchos otros con nombres intraducibles - emitían tonadas durante todo el día. Y las hierbas-plumas y los helechos - cuerdas de violín mágicas, polifonías y lenguas de bronce y ruidos del bosque - y todas las cañas de los estanques blancos como leche continuaban la música, suavemente, inclusive de noche. De hecho allí siempre se oía una música tenue. (*Cuentos desde el Reino Peligroso*, 50)[12]

11. Tolkien, J.R.R., *Roverandom*, ed. Christina Scull and Wayne G. Hammond (London: HarperCollins, 1998).

12. "What sounds there were, were made chiefly by the plants. The flowers – the whitebells, the fairbells and the silverbells, the tinklebells and the ringaroses; the rhymeroyals and the pennywhistles, the tintrumpets and the creamhorns (a very pale cream), and many others with untranslatable names – made tunes all day long. And the feather-grasses and the ferns –

One of the reasons is that, in Spanish, there are not many words for this type of flower. Also, *ringaroses* will be challenging to translate into a word that makes the reader think of the nursery rhyme, and the literal translation of *rhymeroyals* will not resonate with the type of poetic form Tolkien intended.

The same happens with the wordplay of *polyphonies*, related to contrapuntal music, and *Brasstongues* related to 1 Corinthians 13:1. In Spanish, *helechos* is the common name for *Polypodies*, and *lenguas de bronce* does not have a clear biblical meaning as it does in English because *brasstongues*, which recalls the hart's-tongue fern, has many common ways to be named in Spanish.

Even if it is impossible to translate everything into "Standard Spanish," an effort should be made to use words other than the ones in "Peninsular Spanish" exclusively[13]. There were times when the translators chose a higher register when it was unnecessary (as in the next example where the use of *tañían* for *ringing*): "Los bosques estaban llenos de campanitas de

---

fairyfiddlestrings, polyphonies, and brasstongues, and the cracken in the woods – and all the reeds by the milk-white ponds, they kept up the music, softly, even in the night. In fact there was always a faint thin music going on." (*Perilous Realm*, 30).

13. To defend this argument, according to Instituto Cervantes, in 2022, more than 496 million people are native Spanish Speakers but around 43 million lived in Spain (https://cvc.cervantes.es/lengua/anuario/anuario_22/informes_ic/p01.htm). So, the idea of reaching Spanish diversity in the Tolkien translations would aid in breaking the hierarchical relationship between language and those who speak it, as domination through language remains a colonialist practice well into the 21st century (via, for instance, the prescriptive approach of the Real Academia de la Lengua Española). A language is ever-changing, and in order to broaden our own cultural horizons, different words must be introduced from different backgrounds of speakers of the same language and in different dialectal variants coming from different countries. Language can be like metal: if it does not bend, it ends up breaking.

plata; cuando las vio por primera vez todas tañían suavemente al unísono" (50).[14]

In the following example, the use of *rutilante* for *sparkling water* is a high-register term. In Spanish, *brillante*, *centelleante*, or *destellante* are more commonly used than *rutilante*: "Rover se cansó pronto de esperar, así que fue hasta la puerta iluminada y miró a través de las algas. Entonces vio un amplio salón de baile con siete cúpulas y diez mil columnas de coral, iluminado con la magia más pura y lleno de agua caliente y rutilante" (77). [15]

Regarding translating words to do with the weather, the word *borrasca* is used in "Peninsular Spanish." It is a hydrometeorological system that produces storms, so it is understandable why the translators used this word instead of *tormenta*. Nevertheless, it is a double mistake because not only did the translators use a very local word, but they misused it: "Los duendes pueden permanecer un buen rato fuera del agua y cuando hay borrasca juegan a moverse sobre las olas" (87).[16]

Now, when the natural elements can find their way into translation, as readers, we are able to make text-to-self connections like the one between *Roverandom* and the legend of the Moon Rabbit, even if Tolkien did not have the intention to do so. As Mexican readers, it is impossible not to relate this pre-Columbian legend and *Roverandom*, especially when the Man-in-the-Moon insisted to Roverandom not to mess with his

14. "The woods were filled with silverbells all ringing softly together when he first saw them." (*Perilous Realm*, 30).
15. "Rover soon got very tired of waiting, so he walked along to the shining doorway and peeped through the curtains. He was looking into a vast ballroom with seven domes and ten thousand coral pillars, lit with purest magic and filled with warm and sparkling water." (*Perilous Realm*, 66).
16. "Those goblins can live out of the water for a long while, and play in the surf at the water's edge in a storm." (*Perilous Realm*, 79).

white rabbits "¡No te preocupes de los rayos de luna, y no mates mis conejos blancos!" (49).[17] This connection would not have been possible if the *white rabbits* were translated differently from *conejos blancos*. The legend of the Moon Rabbit says that a rabbit lives on the moon, and while doing research, we found that it is a common myth in some parts of Asia. Even if there are variants of the myth in Mexico, one of the most common is about the god Quetzalcoatl, and the other is about the sacrifice of the fifth sun god.[18]

Only some examples were mentioned of how nature was characterized and characters depicted in the Spanish translation of *Roverandom*. There is inherent subjectivity in them because

---

17. "Don't worry the moonbeams, and don't kill my white rabbits!" (*Perilous Realm*, 27).

18. The first legend states that one day Quetzalcoatl decided to come to Earth disguised as a human being. He visited everything and was pleased about it, but stayed too long and at the end of the day, he was very hungry and became sad. He then encountered a rabbit who offered itself to be eaten by Quetzalcóatl. However, he picked up the rabbit and held it high, so that its shadow would be imprinted on the Moon, and everyone would know the sacrifice the rabbit was willing to make. Regarding the one about the birth of the fifth sun god, in the Mexica mythology there is a series of suns. When it was the time for the fifth sun to be born, the gods gathered at Teotihuacan, and they chose Tecciztecatl and Nanahuatzin to offer themselves as a sacrifice. After a series of trials and ceremonies, there was a pyre for a fire sacrifice at the end. Tecciztecatl tried to throw himself into the fire four times, but he could not sacrifice each time. As it was the fifth sun's birth, Tecciztecatl could not try one more time. Then Nanahuatzin was asked by the gods to sacrifice himself, and he did it on the first try. By doing that, he became the fifth sun. Then Tecciztecatl, ashamed of himself, jumped into the pyre and finally succeeded in the fifth try, and a second sun was born. The gods feared the Earth would be very brightly lit, so they threw a rabbit to Tecciztecatl to dim his light, and he became the Moon. Some sources in English that narrate these myths are *The rabbit on the face of the moon: mythology in the mesoamerican tradition* by Alfredo López Austin and *An Illustrated Dictionary of the Gods and Symbols of Ancient Mexico and the Maya* by Mary Miller and Karl Taube.

those are the ones that most caught our attention. Further analysis should be made considering other varieties of Spanish representing speakers from different parts of the world. This is particularly relevant given that the target audience for this work comprises younger readers who are less likely to recognize that it is written in a different dialectal variation, let alone make an effort necessary to bridge the gap that separates them from such diverse texts. While we acknowledge it is unlikely that a new translation may soon be undertaken, we hope it can be soon enough to profit from the boost of the recent wave of new works and renewed editions consequence of the current focus on lesser-known aspects of the *legendarium*.

Bibliography

Berman, Antoine, *La traduction et la lettre ou l'auberge du lointain* (París: Seuil, 1995)

Croft, Janet Brennan, 'Beyond *The Hobbit*: J.R.R. Tolkien's Other Works for Children', *Journal of Tolkien Research*: Vol. 6 : Iss. 2 , Article 9 (2018). <https://scholar.valpo.edu/journaloftolkienresearch/vol6/iss2/>

Hawkins, Emma, 'Tolkien and Dogs, Just Dogs: in Metaphor and Simile', *Mythlore: A Journal of J.R.R. Tolkien, C.S. Lewis, Charles Williams, and Mythopoeic Literature*: Vol. 27: No. 3, Article 17. (2009) <https://dc.swosu.edu/mythlore/vol27/iss3/17>

Lakowski, Romuald I. '"A Wilderness of Dragons": Tolkien's Treatment of Dragons in Roverandom and Farmer Giles of Ham', *Mythlore: A Journal of J.R.R. Tolkien, C.S. Lewis, Charles Williams, and Mythopoeic Literature*: Vol. 34: No. 1 , Article 8. (2015) <https://dc.swosu.edu/mythlore/vol34/iss1/8>

Marchant, Jennifer, 'Doubles at Work: The Three Rovers in J.R.R. Tolkien's Roverandom', *Mythlore: A Journal of J.R.R. Tolkien, C.S. Lewis, Charles Williams, and Mythopoeic Literature*, vol. 38, iss. 1. (2019) <https://dc.swosu.edu/mythlore/vol38/iss1/6>

Scull, Christina and Wayne G. Hammond, 'Introduction', in *Roverandom*, (London: HarperCollins, 1998).

Shippey, Tom, 'Introduction', in *Tales from the Perilous Realm*, (London: HarperCollins, 1997).

Tolkien, J.R.R. *Cuentos desde el reino peligroso* (trad. Ramón Ibero y Luis Domènech, Barcelona: Minotauro, 2012).
--- *Roverandom*, ed. by Christina Scull and Wayne G. Hammond (London: HarperCollins, 1998).
--- *Tales from the Perilous Realm* (London: HarperCollins, 1997).

Caracterización Y representación de la naturaleza en la traducción al Español de *Roverandom*

Martha Celis Mendoza Y Aline Esperanza Maza Vázquez (Trad. Jorge De la Vega)

Los diferentes elementos que involucran la formación de los personajes en cualquier obra literaria, desde sus nombres hasta sus descripciones, y la forma en que se expresan, tienen un impacto definitivo en la recepción de los lectores. Además, si bien la trama impulsa el desarrollo de tales obras, es a través de la descripción que los autores logran transportar a sus audiencias al mundo que están retratando. Esto es especialmente relevante en el caso de los libros de ciencia ficción y fantasía, donde la suspensión de la incredulidad propuesta por Samuel Taylor Coleridge puede tener lugar gracias a la maestría de los escritores. Tal responsabilidad recae en manos del traductor en el caso de obras vertidas a un idioma extranjero. Presentaremos algunos ejemplos relevantes de estas categorías para analizar cómo los traductores superaron esos desafíos en *Roverandom*.

1 - Caracterización

A pesar de ser casi contemporánea a la creación de *El Hobbit*, *Roverandom* no vio la luz pública hasta muchos años después. Esta es quizás una de las razones de la relativa falta de crítica académica y de traducciones a otros idiomas, como es el caso de muchas de las obras de Tolkien. Otra posible razón es que sólo tiene una relación sutil con los mundos y personajes que pertenecen a las obras más canónicas del *Legendarium*, con apenas unas pocas referencias al "Elvenhome y la tierra de Faery" (Shippey 2008, xiv).[1] El escaso número de trabajos académicos sobre *Roverandom* no sólo se debe a su vida pública relativamente corta, apenas un par de décadas desde su primera edición en 1998, sino también a que todavía se considera un cuento dirigido a los hijos de Tolkien, y no es una parte prominente del *Legendarium*; Janet Brennan Croft menciona que "aunque el cuento subyacente comparte la estructura de transgresión, exilio, penitencia y reconciliación del *immram*, se siente fantasioso y 'miniaturizado' de una manera que a Tolkien más tarde llegó a disgustar, y condenó en su ensayo de 1939 'Sobre los cuentos de hadas'" (Croft 2018, 3). Sin embargo, algunos críticos han identificado paralelismos significativos entre algunos de los personajes del texto y los más icónicos del canon más amplio. Sólo un puñado de estudios están dedicados, parcial o exclusivamente, a aspectos de este trabajo; entre ellos el estudio de Romuald Lakowsky sobre el dragón, el estudio de Emma Hawkins sobre la presencia de perros en las obras de Tolkien, y el análisis de Jennifer Marchant de los tres Rovers como el uso que hace Tolkien de "el doble" (en este caso triple, o mejor dicho, un doble "doble", ya que los tres Rovers no comparten espacio).

Para los traductores al español, algunos aspectos suponen un gran desafío. Presentamos aquí algunos ejemplos, entre ellos algunos relacionados con la forma en que se describe la naturaleza en el libro, así como algunos relacionados con la representación de los tres Rovers, junto con otra tríada, la de los tres magos, Artajerjes, Psamathos y el Hombre de la Luna. Existe una más con tres personajes femeninos importantes para

1. Para las citas textuales de obras que no tienen versión en español, la traducción corresponde al traductor a menos que se indique lo contrario.

el desarrollo de la trama: la mamá del niño Dos, su abuela, y la princesa esposa de Artajerjes, pero esa tríada está claramente desequilibrada en términos de caracterización, por lo que debemos dejarla de lado en este análisis.

El título en sí mismo, siendo también el nombre del protagonista, constituye uno de esos enigmas intraducibles, particularmente considerando que se encontrará con dos homónimos durante el curso de sus aventuras. El nombre Rover, como sabemos, fue una *pièce de résistance* en la onomástica canina.[2] Sin embargo, el referente podría resultar obscuro para alguien fuera de la tradición angloparlante. En un foro de idiomas del conocido diccionario en línea Wordreference.com, podemos encontrar la consulta de un traductor confundido a consecuencia de esta cita problemática: "*If Rover needs to relieve tension over a lost bone or a cat that got away*", para lo que el usuario (un hablante no nativo de inglés) planteó la siguiente pregunta: "¿Por qué la primera letra de 'Rover' está escrita en mayúscula? ¿Rover significa perros aquí? Un miembro del foro respondió: "'Rover' (vagabundo) es un nombre muy común para un perro macho y se reconoce instantáneamente como tal, por lo que aquí es equiparable a 'el perro mascota de alguien'. A la mayoría de los perros les gusta 'vagar' (*to rove*) cuando tienen la oportunidad".[3]

Uno de sus significados, "vagabundo", es apropiado para las aventuras lejanas que debe vivir el protagonista de *Roverandom*. Esto se ha adoptado con frecuencia en español, al menos en México, con un tono de broma cuando se le da un nombre a un perro callejero que es bienvenido en la casa,

2. Sorprendentemente, el nombre Rover ni siquiera aparecía entre los cien principales nombres de perros en el sitio web llamado, irónicamente, rover.com.

3. https://forum.wordreference.com/threads/rover.3517351/.

Solovino ("solo vino", inversión de "vino solo"). Sin embargo, el problema es transformar ese nombre cuando ha tenido un dueño anterior. Como explica Jennifer Marchant, "La historia del perro lunar es relativamente breve. Explica que su nombre de 'Rover' le sentaba bien: 'Yo también era Rover' confiesa" (Marchant 2019, 25). "Nunca me quedaba quieto en ningún sitio, ni pertenecí a nadie antes de venir aquí. Desde que era un cachorro no hice otra cosa que escaparme" (*Perilous Realm*, 25).[4] Por lo tanto, el Hombre de la Luna decide llamarlo Roverandom para evitar confusiones. La connotación de la partícula "random" no se puede explicar con una perífrasis, como en el caso de "Rover, el vagabundo", lo cual no plantea ningún problema ya que sólo está implícita en el nombre en inglés pero nunca se explica:

> Yo fui el primer perro que se llamó Rover, el Vagabundo, hace miles de años; por lo tanto, ¡a ti te tuvieron que poner el nombre de Rover después de mí! ¡Yo también era un vagabundo! Nunca me quedaba quieto en un sitio, ni pertenecí a nadie antes de venir aquí. Desde que era un cachorro no hice otra cosa que escaparme. (*Cuentos desde el Reino Peligroso*, 47)[5]

Más adelante, después de que Roverandom se hizo amigo del Rover marino, afirma que tiene derecho al nombre Rover. Por medio de la afirmación del Rover del mar, Tolkien explica

4. "I never would stop anywhere or belong to anyone before I came here. I did nothing but run away from the time I was a puppy" (*Perilous Realm*, 25).
5. "'I was the first dog that was ever called Rover, thousands of years ago—so you must have been called Rover after me! I *was* a Rover too! I never would stop anywhere, or belong to anyone before I came here. I did nothing but run away from the time I was a puppy.'" (*Perilous Realm*, 26-27).

que está usando uno de los otros significados de la palabra, *sea-rover* (pirata); sin embargo, en la traducción al español, se emplea la palabra "pirata" directamente:

> Creo que yo soy el primero de todos los perros que se llaman Rover. Mi primer amo fue un rover, un auténtico vagabundo, un pirata que navegaba con su barco por las aguas del norte; era un barco muy largo, con velas rojas, y en la proa llevaba tallado un dragón, lo llamaban Gusano Rojo, y me gustaba mucho. (*Cuentos desde el Reino Peligroso*, 80)[6]

La estrategia de los traductores de la versión española en cuanto a la onomástica es consistente; donde los nombres tienen un significado semántico, como el *Man-in-the-Moon*, ofrecen la equivalencia de contenido en español, el Hombre de la Luna; en todos los demás casos, deciden mantener los nombres casi exactamente como en el original inglés, haciendo sólo las adaptaciones fonéticas necesarias para que los nombres puedan ser pronunciados, como en el caso de Psamathos, cambiando el fonema *th*, sin español exacto, equivalente a una simple t; las letras "Ps" del principio, se conservan ya que su uso, o no, contribuye a la caracterización de Psámatos, como podemos ver en este ejemplo:

> ¡De modo que has vuelto! Pensé que no tardarías en cansarte del viejo P-sámatos (y bufó para emitir una exagerada P). Él no puede hacerlo todo. Bueno, ¿a qué has venido? Estamos

6. "'I expect I'm the first of all dog Rovers. My first master was a Rover, a real one, a sea-rover who sailed his ship in the northern waters; it was a long ship with red sails, and it was carved like a dragon in the prow, and he called it the Red Worm and loved it.'" (*Perilous Realm*, 70).

en una fiesta y has interrumpido la música. (*Cuentos desde el Reino Peligroso*, 77)[7]

Lo mismo se hace con Artajerjes para hacerlo consistente con la grafía tradicional española del rey persa Jerjes: "—Por favor, señor Ertejerjes, quiero decir, Artajerjes —empezó a decir Rover, más bien atropelladamente y procurando ser muy educado" (*Cuentos desde el Reino Peligroso*, 77). Cabe señalar que en la versión en español, Rover logra pronunciar bien el nombre en su segundo intento, mientras que en el original, se confunde aún más sobre la pronunciación correcta.[8]

Un caso complicado y quizás no tan afortunado es el caso del PAM; las iniciales deben mantenerse probablemente no por la referencia al apodo de Lord Palmerston, como lo mencionan Christine Scull y Wayne C. Hammond, sino también por su calidad fonética, por lo que es imposible que los traductores lo cambien a MAP. Esto provoca la inconsistencia del uso de "el PAM" o "PAM" al usarlo como nombre propio o título, pero también la torpe formulación repetida dos veces en el libro, "en el Pacífico y el Atlántico como Mago". (*Cuentos desde el Reino Peligroso*, 77) "Estaba bastante abrumado por su propia importancia (con extranjeros), desde su matrimonio con la hija del rico rey de los mares, y su destino en el Pacífico y el Atlántico como Mago (la gente lo llamaba en forma abreviada PAM, cuando no estaba delante)—" (*Cuentos desde el Reino*

7. "'So you've turned up! I thought you would get tired of old P-samathos' (how he snorted over that exaggerated P) 'before long. He can't do quite everything. Well, what have you come down here for? We are just having a party, and you're interrupting the music.'" (*Perilous Realm*, 65).
8. "'Please, Mr Arterxaxes, I mean, Ertaxarxes,' began Rover, rather flustered and trying to be very polite." (*Perilous Realm*, 65).

Peligroso, 77).[9] Si bien la descripción de Artajerjes podría recordarnos a Tom Bombadil, la de su esposa, también conocida como Princesa Pam, podría igualmente resonar en nuestros oídos como la de Baya de Oro. Por otro lado, al considerar el uso de un lenguaje elevado, como se menciona en la introducción de Scull y Hammond, se debe tener en cuenta la afirmación de Tolkien en una de sus cartas: "'Un buen vocabulario', escribió una vez (abril de 1959), 'no se adquiere leyendo libros escritos de acuerdo con el criterio que alguien tenga del vocabulario de determinado grupo de edad. Se adquiere leyendo libros que estén por sobre el propio nivel." (Scull y Hammond 1998, 24). Podemos ver un ejemplo aquí con la palabra "monsergas", y la palabra "galimatías" en los siguientes fragmentos, ambos correspondientes a los "*rigmaroles*" originales: "Venga la explicación, y que sea corta; no tengo tiempo para largos galimatías" (*Cuentos desde el Reino Peligroso*, 77).[10]

> En este momento, Artajerjes estaba sentado a su lado, y tuviera o no tuviera tiempo para largas monsergas, estaba escuchando la de su esposa. O la había estado escuchando antes de que apareciera Rover. La señora Artajerjes puso fin a su monserga y a su costura, tan pronto como vio a Rover, y tras deslizarse hacia abajo lo capturó y lo llevó al asiento. (*Cuentos desde el Reino Peligroso*, 78)[11]

9. "He had become rather full of his own importance (with strangers), since his marriage to the rich mer-king's daughter, and his appointment to the post of Pacific and Atlantic Magician (the PAM, they called him for short, when he was not present)." (*Perilous Realm*, 65-66).

10. "'Get on to the explanation, and make it short; I've no time for long rigmaroles.'" (*Perilous Realm*, 65).

11. "Artaxerxes was at the moment sitting beside her, and whether he had the time or not for long rigmaroles, he was listening to one of her wife's- Or had been, before Rover turned up. Mrs Artaxerxes put an end to her rigmarole,

La versión española incluso proporciona dos términos diferentes de registro alto para uno solo en el original, quizás con la intención de evitar la tendencia deformativa de homogeneización, identificada por Antoine Berman al sobrecompensar, introduciendo una variedad más amplia de términos: "*Elle consiste a unifier sur tous les plans le tissu de l'original, alors que celui-ci est originairement hétérogène [...] un tendance en soi, qui plonge profondément ses racines dans l'être du traducteur.*" (Berman 95, 60).[12] Es un hecho reconocido que uno de los objetivos de la literatura infantil es la adquisición del lenguaje y la expansión semántica, y en esto definitivamente destaca *Roverandom.*

2 - Representación de la Naturaleza

Las notas de Scull y Hammond para la primera edición de Roverandom son fundamentales para comprender el juego de palabras de la historia. Desafortunadamente, la versión que aparece en *Cuentos desde el Reino Peligroso* no las incluye, y si en inglés esto podría causar algunos problemas, en la traducción al español se pierden muchas cosas porque no tienen sentido.

El primer ejemplo que mencionaremos es el juego de palabras que hace Tolkien con los sonidos y las descripciones de las flores en el segundo capítulo. Tolkien hace un símil utilizando nombres e instrumentos musicales que no aparece

---

and to her sockmending, as soon as she caught sight of him, and floating down picked him up and carried him back to her couch." (*Perilous Realm*, 67).

12. "Consiste en unifica, en todos los planos, el tejido del original, mientras que éste es originalmente heterogéneo. [...] una tendencia en sí misma, profundamente arraigada en el ser del traductor" (Trad. Martha Celis).

en la traducción al español, e incluso se trunca aprovechando las palabras del propio Tolkien: "y muchos otros con nombres intraducibles":

> Los ruidos que había, venían sobre todo de las plantas. Las flores —las campanas blancas, las campanas claras y las campanas de plata, las campanas tintineantes y las trompetitas y los cuernos de crema (una crema muy pálida) y muchos otros con nombres intraducibles— emitían tonadas durante todo el día. Y las hierbas-plumas y los helechos —cuerdas de violín mágicas, polifonías y lenguas de bronce y ruidos del bosque— y todas las cañas de los estanques blancos como leche continuaban la música, suavemente, inclusive de noche. De hecho, allí siempre se oía una música tenue. (*Cuentos desde el Reino Peligroso*, 50).[13]

Una de las razones es que, en español, no hay muchas palabras para este tipo de flor. Además, las *ringaroses* serían difíciles de traducir a una palabra que haga pensar al lector en la canción infantil, y la traducción literal de *rhymeroyals* (iris) no resonará con el tipo de forma poética que Tolkien pretendía.

Lo mismo sucede con el juego de palabras de *polyphonies*, relacionado con la música contrapuntística, y *Brasstongues* relacionado con 1 Corintios 13:1. En español, *helechos* es el

13. "What sounds there were, were made chiefly by the plants. The flowers – the whitebells, the fairbells and the silverbells, the tinklebells and the ringaroses; the rhymeroyals and the pennywhistles, the tintrumpets and the creamhorns (a very pale cream), and many others with untranslatable names – made tunes all day long. And the feather-grasses and the ferns – fairyfiddlestrings, polyphonies, and brasstongues, and the cracken in the woods – and all the reeds by the milk-white ponds, they kept up the music, softly, even in the night. In fact there was always a faint thin music going on." (*Perilous Realm*, 30).

nombre común de *Polypodies*, y *lenguas de bronce* no tiene un significado bíblico claro como lo tiene en inglés porque *brasstongues*, que recuerda al helecho lengua de ciervo, tiene muchas formas comunes de nombrarse en español.

Si bien es imposible traducirlo todo al español estándar, se debe hacer un esfuerzo por utilizar palabras distintas a las del español peninsular exclusivamente.[14] Hubo momentos en que los traductores eligieron un registro más alto cuando no era necesario (como en el siguiente ejemplo donde emplean *tañían* para *sonar*): "Los bosques estaban llenos de campanitas de plata; cuando las vio por primera vez todas tañían suavemente al unísono." (*Cuentos desde el Reino Peligroso*, 50).[15]

En el siguiente ejemplo, el empleo del término "rutilante" para *sparkling water* es un término de registro alto. En español, palabras como brillante, centelleante o destellante se usan más comúnmente que rutilante.: "Rover se cansó pronto de esperar, así que fue hasta la puerta iluminada y miró a través de las algas. Entonces vio un amplio salón de baile con siete cúpulas y diez mil columnas de coral, iluminado con la magia más pura

14. Para defender este argumento, según el Instituto Cervantes, en 2022, más de 496 millones de personas son hispanohablantes nativos pero sólo alrededor de 43 millones vivían en España (https://cvc.cervantes.es/lengua/anuario/anuario_22/informes_ic/p01.htm). Así pues, la idea de alcanzar la diversidad del español en las traducciones de Tolkien ayudaría a romper la relación jerárquica entre la lengua y quienes la hablan, ya que la dominación a través de la lengua sigue siendo una práctica colonialista hasta bien entrado el siglo XXI (a través, por ejemplo, del enfoque prescriptivo de la Real Academia de la Lengua Española). Una lengua está en constante cambio y, para ampliar nuestros propios horizontes culturales, hay que introducir palabras diferentes procedentes de distintos orígenes de hablantes de la misma lengua y en distintas variantes dialectales procedentes de distintos países. La lengua puede ser como el metal: si no se dobla, acaba rompiéndose.

15. "The woods were filled with silverbells all ringing softly together when he first saw them." (*Perilous Realm*, 30).

y lleno de agua caliente y rutilante." (*Cuentos desde el Reino Peligroso*, 77).[16]

En cuanto a la traducción de palabras relacionadas con el tiempo meteorológico, en el español peninsular se utiliza la palabra "borrasca". Es un sistema hidrometeorológico que produce tormentas, por lo que se comprende por qué los traductores usaron esta palabra en lugar de "tormenta". Sin embargo, es un doble error porque los traductores no solo usaron una palabra muy local, sino que la usaron de manera incorrecta.: "Los duendes pueden permanecer un buen rato fuera del agua y cuando hay borrasca juegan a moverse sobre las olas." (*Cuentos desde el Reino Peligroso*, 87).[17]

Ahora, cuando los elementos naturales pueden encontrar su camino hacia la traducción, como lectores, somos capaces de hacer conexiones entre el texto y uno mismo, como la que existe entre *Roverandom* y la leyenda del Conejo Lunar, incluso si Tolkien no tenía la intención de hacerlo. Como lectores mexicanos, es imposible no relacionar esta leyenda precolombina y Roverandom, sobre todo cuando el Hombre de la Luna le insiste a Roverandom que no se meta con sus conejos blancos.: "¡No te preocupes de los rayos de luna, y no mates mis conejos blancos!" (*Cuentos desde el Reino Peligroso*, 49).[18] Esta conexión no habría sido posible si los white rabbits se tradujeran de manera diferente a "conejos blancos". La leyenda del Conejo Lunar dice que un conejo vive en la luna y, durante

16. "Rover soon got very tired of waiting, so he walked along to the shining doorway and peeped through the curtains. He was looking into a vast ballroom with seven domes and ten thousand coral pillars, lit with purest magic and filled with warm and sparkling water." (*Perilous Realm*, 66).

17. "Those goblins can live out of the water for a long while, and play in the surf at the water's edge in a storm." (*Perilous Realm*, 79).

18. "Don't worry the moonbeams, and don't kill my white rabbits!" (*Perilous Realm*, 27).

la investigación, nos dimos cuenta de que es un mito común en algunas partes de Asia. Si bien existen variantes del mito en México, una de las más comunes es sobre el dios Quetzalcóatl, y la otra es sobre el sacrificio del Quinto Sol.[19]

Sólo se mencionaron algunos ejemplos de cómo se caracterizó la naturaleza y se representaron los personajes en la traducción al español de *Roverandom*. Hay una subjetividad inherente en ellos porque son los que más llamaron nuestra atención. Es importante llevar a cabo un análisis más profundo que tome en consideración otras variedades de la lengua española que representen a personas de diferentes partes del mundo. Esto es particularmente relevante dado que el público de dicha obra comprende lectores más jóvenes que

19. La primera leyenda cuenta que un día Quetzalcóatl decidió venir a la Tierra disfrazado de ser humano. Lo visitó todo y se alegró de ello, pero se quedó demasiado tiempo y al final del día tenía mucha hambre y se puso triste. Entonces se encontró con un conejo que se ofreció para que Quetzalcóatl se lo comiera. Sin embargo, tomó al conejo y lo sostuvo en alto, para que su sombra quedara impresa en la Luna y todos supieran el sacrificio que el conejo estaba dispuesto a hacer. En cuanto a la del nacimiento del quinto dios solar, en la mitología mexica hay una serie de soles. Cuando llegó el momento de que naciera el quinto sol, los dioses se reunieron en Teotihuacan y eligieron a Tecciztecatl y Nanahuatzin para que se ofrecieran en sacrificio. Tras una serie de pruebas y ceremonias, al final se hizo una pira para un sacrificio de fuego. Tecciztecatl intentó arrojarse al fuego cuatro veces, pero no pudo sacrificarse cada vez. Como era el nacimiento del quinto sol, Tecciztecatl no pudo intentarlo una vez más. Entonces los dioses pidieron a Nanahuatzin que se sacrificara, y lo hizo al primer intento. Al hacerlo, se convirtió en el quinto sol. Entonces Tecciztecatl, avergonzado de sí mismo, saltó a la pira y finalmente tuvo éxito en el quinto intento, y nació un segundo sol. Los dioses temían que la Tierra estuviera muy iluminada, así que arrojaron un conejo a Tecciztecatl para atenuar su luz, y éste se convirtió en la Luna. Algunas fuentes en inglés que narran estos mitos son *The rabbit on the face of the moon: mythology in the mesoamerican tradition* de Alfredo López Austin y *An Illustrated Dictionary of the Gods and Symbols of Ancient Mexico and the Maya* de Mary Miller y Karl Taube.

son menos propensos a reconocer cuando un texto está escrito en una variación dialectal diferente, y mucho menos a hacer el esfuerzo necesario para cerrar la brecha que los separa de textos tan diversos. Si bien reconocemos que es poco probable que se lleve a cabo una nueva traducción pronto, esperamos que pueda ser lo suficientemente pronto como para beneficiarse del impulso de la reciente ola de nuevos trabajos y ediciones renovadas, consecuencia del enfoque actual en aspectos menos conocidos del *legendarium*.

From the Black Gate to the Kṛṣṇā Dvāra: on the curious resonances of Swami Mudrikancha

Sonali Arvind Chunodkar

One offshoot of the popularity of Peter Jackson's *The Lord of the Rings* trilogy in India was the publication of the Marathi-language[1] translations of J.R.R. Tolkien's *The Hobbit* and *The Lord of the Rings* by Meena Kinikar and Mugdha Karnik, respectively. This paper restricts itself to an overview of select aspects of Karnik's three-volume Marathi translation of *The Lord of the Rings* published in 2015 and titled *Swami*

1. Marathi is one of the twenty-two languages listed in the Eighth Schedule of the Constitution of India and is the official language of the state of Maharashtra. Marathi, like Hindi and Sanskrit, is currently written in the Devanagari script, albeit in the Balbodh mode. However, this was not the case until the 1950s before which Marathi was also written in the Modi script. As Pushkar Sohoni points out, it was only after "the *Report of the Official Language Commission* (1956) recommended the adoption of Devanagari for all languages in India, particularly for the 'daughter languages of Sanskrit, Hindi, Bengali, Marathi, and Gujarati'" that "the teaching of the Modi script was unceremoniously discontinued in schools from about 1959 onwards, and students learned Marathi in Devanagari alone" (2016, 19). For insightful historical overviews of the standardization process of Marathi and its writing script(s) since British colonial times, see Dilip Chavan (2013) and Sohoni (2016), respectively. It must also be noted here that India does not have any national language as such, though it does have two official languages - Hindi and English. In addition to these languages, G.N. Devy, who heads the People's Linguistic Survey of India project, identified around 780 languages that are spoken in India (see Roychowdhury 2020). The reduced socio-cultural, economic, and political value ascribed to most - if not all - of these languages continues to threaten their very survival.

Mudrikancha - Mudrikeche Sathidar, *Te Don Manore*, and *Rajache Punaragaman*.[2]

The first section offers a glimpse into Karnik's avowed motivations for translating Tolkien's work; it lists select aspects of his work that caught her interest along with those that she dismissed out of disinterest. The second section provides select examples of the trace left on the quality of the translation by her disinterest in the historical dimension of Tolkien's fictional world. This section includes a short report on the parts of Tolkien's text that are excluded in the translation. It also offers select examples where, conversely, the translator included more details. The third section undertakes a comparative examination of the translation's word and stylistic choices. The final section foregrounds the curious, jarring cultural evocations brought about by the translator's word choices in connection with her dismissal of a crucial aspect of Tolkien's fantasy fiction - its philosophical, theological dimension.

1 - The Reluctant Translator

It can be discerned from the quality of the Marathi translation of *The Lord of the Rings* that the translator displays hardly any in-depth familiarity with the stories included in *The Silmarillion* or with Tolkien's other fictional and scholarly writings. In fact, she repeatedly indicates that she had no interest in *The Hobbit* and *The Lord of the Rings* beyond the translation exercise itself. In interviews published upon the release of *Swami Mudrikancha*, in the translator's introduction, and in a Marathi blog post titled 'Anuvāda Karatānā' (While Translating), Karnik points out that

2. Except for the book titles of Tolkien's translated works, this paper follows the IAST conventions for transliterating the Devanagari script into the Latin one.

she undertook the task of translating Tolkien's work only upon her daughter's insistence, who in turn is a Tolkien fan (Joshi 2015; Chanda-Vaz 2015; Karnik 2015, ix-x, xi, xiv). Unlike Nilesh Pashte, the publisher, and Kinikar, Karnik emphasizes that she felt the need to read Tolkien's work only twice (2015, xiv; Collier 2011; Chanda-Vaz 2015).[3] She compares this to the estimated sixteen and ten prior readings she had undertaken for what she found to be the more challenging, taxing task of translating Ayn Rand's *Atlas Shrugged* and *The Fountainhead*, respectively (2015, x; 2016; Joshi 2015; Chanda-Vaz 2015).

Furthermore, she makes it a point to specify that her interest in translating Tolkien's work was restricted to its narrative style ("kathanaśailī"), its adventure story ("sāhasakathā"), and its descriptions of nature (2015, 10; 2016). She makes no bones about her aversion towards its technology-opposed worldview ("taṃtrajñāna virodha") (2015, 10). She explicitly states her disinterest in any in-depth or scholarly engagement with Tolkien's work and in conveying any of its philosophical underpinnings or themes ("tattvajñāna") (2015, 10, 13). Indeed, she does not allow even the possibility that *The Lord of the Rings* might have any such philosophical underpinning or theme worth conveying in the first place (2016). This misplaced belief finds expression in the following revealing mistranslation that reduces Celeborn's cautionary statement concerning the possibility of the transmission of useful information, truth, and even wisdom through folklore into one that is concerned solely with such lore's capacity to safeguard old words and their meanings from the ravages of time:

3. She first read the book during a period of illness (around the years 1999-2000) upon the insistence of her children; her second reading was in 2013 when she decided to undertake the translation project (Karnik 2015, ix-x). She began working on the translation in April 2013 and completed all three volumes in September 2014 (Karnik 2015, x; Chanda-Vaz 2015).

"Maga mī āṇakhī kāhī sāṃgāyacī garajaca nāhī," Silebôrna[4] mhaṇālā, "paṇa prācīna kālāpāsūna cālata ālelyā junyā ākhyāyikāṃnā agadīca dhutakārū nakosa, kāraṇa anekadā aśāca bhākaḍakathāṃtūna junyā kālacyā jāṇatyā lokāṃnī ekekālī vāparalele śabda āṇi tyāṃce artha jivaṃta rākhale jātāta." (*Mudrikeche Sathidar*, 536)

"Then I do not need to say anything more," Celeborn said, "but don't completely, scornfully reject the legends that have endured since ancient times, since often it is through such irrelevant stories that words which were once used by knowledgeable people of olden times and their meanings have been kept alive." (Provisional translation, mine)[5]

2 - A Wanting Translation

In her Marathi blog post, Karnik also confesses that she became weary of translating the poems which disclose the historical dimension of Tolkien's fictional world (2016). However, she does admit her dissatisfaction with her translated versions (2016). The trace that the translator's disinterest left on the quality of the translation comes to the fore in the many mistranslations

4. While the possibility of misrendering the pronunciation of names and phrases in Tolkien's constructed languages has been mitigated by resources like Jackson's trilogies, some instances remain (e.g., Eregion ["Irijana"], Oromë ["Ôroma"]) (*Mudrikeche Sathidar*, 63; *Rajache Punaragaman*, 132). Unlike English, such errors are more visible/audible in Marathi because of the comparatively greater grapheme–phoneme correspondence of its writing system.

5. The corresponding sentences in Tolkien's work are "'Then I need say no more,' said Celeborn. 'But do not despise the lore that has come down from distant years; for oft it may chance that old wives keep in memory word of things that once were needful for the wise to know'" (*FR*, 'Farewell to Lórien', 374).

dealing with specific aspects that touch upon Tolkien's history of Middle-earth. This paper restricts itself to considering only two examples from the many available in the text.

The first one deals with the exact nature of familial relation between characters: Hamfast Gamgee starts out as Sam's 'father' (*bāpa*) only to be subsequently addressed as his 'grandfather' (*ājobā* and *ājjā*) before returning to being his 'father' further on in the work (see *Mudrikeche Sathidar*, 27, 88, 96, 518). Hamfast, along with a few older hobbits like Bilbo, is also frequently addressed as *buḍhḍhā* - a word derisively used for and meaning an 'old man' - particularly in the earlier parts of the work instead of the comparatively neutral *mhātārā* (old man). The latter is also a colloquial term for one's father, and the later parts of the translation employs this term to indicate Sam's relation to Hamfast. Furthermore, the latter is often described as being a *baḍabaḍyā* (chatterbox), even though Tolkien's text does not specifically mention this sense or trait (see *Mudrikeche Sathidar*, 26, cf. *FR*, 'A Long-expected Party', 22). Perhaps it is the translator's uncertain understanding of the word 'gaffer' that results in this added character trait and Hamfast's shifting relationship with Sam.[6]

The second example involves the much-valued status of kingship in Tolkien's work: the significance of Aragorn's claim to the kingship of both Gondor and Arnor gets severely undermined by the translation's indiscriminate use of the words *rājā* (king) and *mahārāja* (great king/sovereign). For instance, Éomer addresses Aragorn as "mahārāja" in place of "lord" when the latter is still in pursuit of Pippin and Merry and the orcs who had captured them (*Te Don Manore*, 35; *TT*, 'The

6. For example, J.T. Molesworth's dictionary defines the word *ājobā* as "a respectful term of compellation or mention for a grandfather or an old man; gaffer" (1857, 64).

Riders of Rohan', 434). In this very chapter, Éomer himself is addressed as *mahārāja*, while Théoden is called a mere *rājā*:

> "Vela saṃpata cālalāya," to Svāra Êragôrnakaḍe lakṣa na detā bolū lāgalā, "āpaṇa tvarene dakṣiṇelā gela pāhije, *mahārāja*. Yā rānaṭī lokāṃnā tyāṃcyā kalpanāṃcyā rājyāta ramū deta. Kiṃvā maga tyāṃnā bāṃdhūna ghālā āṇi *rājākaḍe* gheūna calā." (*Te Don Manore*, 36; emphasis added)

> "Time is running out," that Rider started speaking without heeding Aragorn, "we must go southwards immediately, *great king*. Let these wild folk remain absorbed in their realm of imagination. Or else have them bound and taken to the *king*." (Provisional translation, mine)[7]

Beren is similarly styled as a king's son or prince ("rājaputra" and "rājayuvā") in Aragorn's tale of Tinúviel (*Mudrikeche Sathidar*, 271, 273; cf. *FR*, 'A Knife in the Dark', 191-3). Even Galadriel, titled as 'Lady' in Tolkien, is addressed as *rāṇī* (queen) and *mahārāṇī* (great or chief queen) throughout. Consequently, the translation has to take recourse to the word "Svāminī" (lady, mistress) in the crucial passage in which Galadriel envisions what she would become (i.e., "a Queen") if she were to take the One Ring offered by Frodo (*Mudrikeche Sathidar*, 422; *FR*, 'The Mirror of Galadriel', 366).

The translation also excludes a few of the individual words, phrases, sentences, footnotes, and passages present in Tolkien's main narrative text. In fact, all three volumes contain

7. The corresponding sentences in Tolkien are "'Time is pressing,' said the Rider, not heeding Aragorn. 'We must hasten south, lord. Let us leave these wild folk to their fancies. Or let us bind them and take them to the king'" (*TT*, 'The Riders of Rohan', 434-5).

at least one missing passage (see 'The Shadow of the Past', 62; 'The Window on the West', 665; 'The Land of Shadow', 926; cf. *Mudrikeche Sathidar*, 87; *Te Don Manore*, 366; *Rajache Punaragaman*, 257). As far as the appendices are concerned, Appendix A replaces Tolkien's text with summarized accounts in some places while completely overlooking the existence of his explanatory footnotes. Appendix B is reduced to very brief summaries of the three Ages; it also dispenses with the detailed chronologies present in the English text. Appendices C, D, E, and F are absent in the translated work. The translator only lists their contents and recommends interested readers to refer to Tolkien's English work instead (*Rajache Punaragaman*, 460). The exclusion of Appendix C containing the helpful 'Family Trees' of the principal hobbit characters is particularly unfortunate.

Conversely, there are other instances where the translation describes certain actions and objects in more detail compared to Tolkien's text. To give one example,[8] the word "slain" in Tolkien's work takes on the additional gory imagery evoked by the word *kaṃṭhasnāna* (throat-ablution), which is "a covert term for cutting the throat" that places emphasis on the victim's body getting bathed in the flowing blood (Molesworth 1857, 127):

> Tyāmule tyaṃnā yā nāṭyācā śevaṭacā aṃka disalā nāhī - Uglukalā jaṃgalācyā agadī sīmevaraca tyā Ghoḍesvārāṃnī gāṭhala hota āṇi titheca Eomerane, Mārkacyā Tisaryā Senānāyakāne, ghoḍyāvarūna khālī utarūna tyācyāśī talavārīne

8. Other examples include the translation of Sam's "brown" hands into 'tanned' ("rāpalelā," "rāpalelyā") ones (*TT*, 'The Stairs of Cirith Ungol', 714; *RK*, 'The Tower of Cirith Ungol', 915; *Te Don Manore*, 438; *Rajache Punaragaman*, 241).

laḍhāī karūna tyālā akhera *kaṃṭhasnāna* ghātala. (*Te Don Manore*, 73; emphasis added)

So it was that they did not see the last act of this play - Uglúk was overtaken by those Horsemen at the very edge of the forest and it was there that Éomer, Third Commander of the Mark, after dismounting and engaging in a sword fight with him, finally gave him a *throat-bath* [slit his throat]. (Provisional translation, mine)[9]

3 - A Translated World of Many Words

Karnik states that her primary concern while translating was to live up to the challenge of the grandeur (*vaibhava*), elegance (*lālitya*), power (*tākada*), and beauty (*sauṃdarya*) of Tolkien's language use in *The Lord of the Rings* (2015, ix, xiv; 2016). She also proclaims her love for the Marathi and English languages and her pride in the former's vocabularic range, which is enriched by Sanskrit, Prakrit,[10] Old Marathi, Persian,[11] Hindi, and English among other languages, as well as in her own mastery over the language (see 2015, xi-xii; 2016; Chanda-Vaz 2015). One of the ways of displaying this rightly claimed linguistic command is through the translation's deployment of several synonyms for signifying a single referent. Tolkien, on the other hand, signifies the same referent through one or two

9. The corresponding sentences in Tolkien are "So it was that they did not see the last stand, when Uglúk was overtaken and brought to bay at the very edge of Fangorn. There he was slain at last by Éomer, the Third Marshal of the Mark, who dismounted and fought him sword to sword" (*TT*, 'The Uruk-Hai', 459).

10. For introductory information on Prakrit, see Anando Ghosh (2020).

11. For an encyclopaedic entry on the Perso-Arabic influence on Marathi, see S.H. Qasemi and *EIr* (2013).

more commonly and consistently used words. For example, the word 'ranger(s)' in Tolkien's work is translated variously as *phirastā*, *kṣetrapāla*, *reṃjarsa*, *bhaṭake*, *bhaṭake reṃjarsa*, and *bhaṭake śipāī*.[12] The presence of such vocabularic variety poses an obstacle in engaging younger - particularly teenage - readers because of the translation's resulting comparatively complicated language constructions. It also ends up confusing many first-time readers of Tolkien's work regardless of their age group because of such oft-changing signifiers.

One also comes across several compound-word formations of an archaic bent that rely on either Sanskrit loanwords (*tatsama*) or Sanskritized Marathi. These word formations are best seen in the translated descriptions of the natural world. Unfortunately, the translation gets mired in avoidable errors in the process. For example, the "waning moon" in Tolkien's work becomes "śuklendu" or the 'waxing moon' in the translation (*FR*, 'Lothlórien', 337; *Mudrikeche Sathidar*, 479).[13] The use of *aruṇodaya* for 'dawn' with its allusion to Aruna, a male solar deity in Hindu mythology, bolsters the translation's continued reference to the sun as 'he' in keeping with Marathi grammatical gender prescriptions (*Te Don Manore*, 230, 416). It thereby clashes with Tolkien's account of Arien and his use of the pronoun "she" to refer to the sun (*Silmarillion*, 110-3; *FR*, 'At the Sign of the Prancing Pony', 160).

Some errors also appear in the translations of time units through archaic time measuring divisions, such as *prahara*

12. The etymological roots of these words are in Persian, Sanskrit, English, and Hindi.

13. While *śukla* means "light" or "bright" and refers to "the waxing half of the month or of any lunar day in it," *iṃdu* is a Sanskrit loanword and "is said to mean in the Veda a drop of Soma juice, a bright drop or spark" in addition to being one of the names of the moon god in Hindu mythology (Molesworth 1857, 795; Apte 1890, 276).

for 'hour', *ghaṭakā* for both 'hour' and "middle morning," and *uṣaḥkāla* for 'morning' (*RK*, 'The Siege of Gondor', 818). While one *prahara* amounts to three hours, one *ghaṭakā* measures to twenty-four minutes. *Uṣaḥkāla* refers to the period of two *ghaṭakā* before sunrise and alludes to the Vedic goddess of dawn (i.e., Ushas). The translation could have easily avoided these errors by sticking with more commonly used words - not just in general but also elsewhere in the translation - like *tāsa* (hour), *pahāṭa* (dawn), and *sakāla* (morning). The translations of the units of measuring length and depth, on the other hand, are often carefully thought out: for example, the translator substitutes equivalent measuring units like *vāra* and *puruṣa* in place of units like 'yards' or 'ells' and 'fathoms', respectively, and provides exact or approximate conversions in each case.

Another promising feature of the translation is its use of the familiar form of the second person pronoun (*tū*). This use has helped convey to a great extent the sense of "the strangeness of Hobbit-speech" (*RK*, Appendix F, II, 1133). However, the translation's pronominal choices in this connection do not always follow Tolkien's observations. For example, Sam addresses only Frodo in the equivalent deferential form of the second person pronoun (*tumhī*) throughout.[14] Tolkien, on the other hand, specifies that the deferential form "lingered only among the villagers, especially of the Westfarthing, who used them as endearments" (1133). The translation's word and stylistic choices nonetheless go some way towards bringing about the effect of encountering the different speech styles often used by "Hobbits such as Frodo, and other persons such as Gandalf and Aragorn" (1133).

The translator also puts in much effort to localize or naturalize Tolkien's work for Marathi readership. As she

14. The comparatively more formal deferential form in Marathi (*āpaṇa*) does not appear anywhere in the translation.

mentions in a published interview and in her translator's introduction, the verse "haritatṛṇāṃcyā makhamālīvara" in her translation of Tom Bombadil's poem alludes to Balkavi's well-known poem *Phularāṇī* written in around 1911 and the tradition of Marathi nature poetry (Joshi 2015; Karnik 2015, xi; *Mudrikeche Sathidar*, 177). The translated poem consequently departs to some extent from Tolkien's verse as can be discerned from the following lines:

Tyā ḍohācyā kāṭhāvaratī
prathama gavasalī hotī majalā
hī suṃdaraśī Nadīkanyā
'haritatṛṇāṃcyā makhamālīvara'[15]
basalī hotī sonaparī
suṃdara mājhī Golḍaberī (*Mudrikeche Sathidar*, 177)

On the banks of that pool
I had first found
this beautiful River-daughter
On a velvet of green grass
was seated this gold-fairy
my beautiful Goldberry (Provisional translation, mine)[16]

---

15. The verse reproduces the second of the first four lines of Balkavi's poem:

Hirave hirave gāra gālice
harita tṛṇācyā makhamālīce;
tyā suṃdara makhamālīvaratī
phularāṇī hī khelata hotī! (2011, 30)

Green, greenish carpets
of the velvet of green grass;
upon that beautiful velvet
this queen of flowers was playing! (Provisional translation, mine)

16. The corresponding lines in Tolkien are "*By that pool long ago I found the River-daughter, | fair young Goldberry sitting in the rushes*" (*FR*, 'In the House of Tom Bombadil', 126).

The inclusion of this allusion, however, would greatly appeal to Marathi readers. It also echoes Tolkien's own verbatim reproduction of the line, "the cow jumped over the Moon," from the popular nursery rhyme and his engagement with the tradition of the Man in the Moon (*FR*, 'At the Sign of the Prancing Pony', 159).

The translated ring verse, on the other hand, places greater emphasis on its sound patterns:[17]

Nabhākhālacyā Elphanṛpāṃcyā Tīna Mudrikā
pāṣāṇācyā bhavya dālanī Ḍvārphanṛpāṃcyā Sāta Mudrikā
mṛtyūbhayākula Martya Mānavāṃsāṭhī ghaḍalyā Naū Mudrikā
āṇi Ekaca - kevala Ekaca
Kṛṣṇa Śaktīcyā Svāmīkaritā
jo asela ārūḍha aghora kālyā siṃhāsanāvara
tamasāṃkita kālyā [...] *Morḍôracyā Maraṇabhūmīvara* [...]
hī Eka Mudrikā aṃkuśa jaisā sarvāṃvaracā
hī Eka Mudrikā gheīla śodha sarvāṃcā
hī Eka Mudrikā gheīla vedha sarvāṃcā
hī Ekaca ghālīla sakalāṃnā, vilakhā tamapāśāṃcā ..
tamasāṃkita kālyā [...] *Morḍaôracyā Maraṇabhūmīvara*
(*Mudrikeche Sathidar*, 68-9)[18]

This recourse to alliteration along with the translator's greater reliance on Sanskrit loanwords and Sanskritized vocabulary

17. For an insightful account on Tolkien's views on "'phonaesthetic pleasure' (*Letters*: Letter 144, 176)," see Dimitra Fimi (2010, 80, 69-115).

18. The translated version thematizes the notion of death by understanding "Mortal Men" as fearing death ("*mṛtyūbhayākula*"), by calling Mordor a land of death ("*Maraṇabhūmīvara*") rather than one where "the Shadows lie," and by alluding ("vilakhā tamapāśāṃcā") to the noose-like weapon of Yama (i.e., the *Yamapasha*), who functions as the god of death in Hindu and Buddhist mythologies (*FR*, 'The Shadow of the Past', 50; *Mudrikeche Sathidar*, 68-9).

marks its thematic and stylistic closeness to the genre of *adbhuta kādambarī* or the Marathi fantastic, marvellous novel[19] as compared to classic works of mythological fiction in Marathi like V.S. Khandekar's 1959 novel *Yayāti.*[20]

Khandekar's feted novel also features Sanskritized vocabulary, which is in keeping with its mythological subject, although it does not completely eschew words of Perso-Arabic etymology. However, it displays consistently used word choices, comparatively shorter sentences along with a conversational,

---

19. Cf. the emphasis on alliteration in the following prose sentence from Naro Sadashiv Risbud's *Manjughosha* (1868):

Majhya ishta kanyene nrupshreshtha kumaraas shishta janahi santushta houn jyaas maan tukavitil ashaa ashtavivahaatil varishtha gaandharva vivahe karun varron tee yatheshta sukhopabhogaanubhav ghenar, to yaa dushtamati streene kevel eknishtha saapatna va matsarbhaavaane tijavar mahaa aarishta anave asaa hetu dhaarana karoonach majhe manaat tijavishayi klishta kalpana bharavoon rushta anta; karanaane tijalaa naanaa kashta bhogaavayaas lavoon nashta dashes laavile he spashta aahe. (quoted in Jaaware 2002, 75)

As noted elsewhere, other characteristic features of the *adbhuta kādambarī* include "a highly Sanskritic style and rhetorical features of Sanskrit narratives," "exciting incidents and moralization," "coincidences bordering on miracles," and "long and elaborate descriptions" (Das 1991, 198; see Jaaware 2002; Chunodkar 2021).

20. Khandekar's Sahitya Akademi Award (1960) as well as Jnanpith Award (1974) winning Marathi novel is an imaginative, fictional retelling of a minor episode in the *Mahabharata* concerning the tale of Yayāti. It traces the life of Yayāti, first as the prince and subsequently as the king of Hastināpūra. It dwells over the formative incidents in his childhood that resulted in his excessive pursuit of physical pleasure and his fear of death, along with all his guilt-ridden choices leading to his being fatally cursed with untimely old age. It is particularly concerned with his relationships with women, including Devayānī (his brahmin wife and the daughter of the guru of the Asūra) and Śarmiṣṭhā (a kshatriya princess and daughter of the Daitya king Vṛṣaparvā; later Devayānī's maidservant and Yayāti's lover/wife). The novel switches between the point of view of these three narrators.

confessional style of narration as can be discerned from the following passages:

> Pipinalā jhopa lāgū lāgalī tevhā tyālā eka vegalīca saṃvedanā jāṇavata hotī. To āṇi Gênḍālpha jaṇū ekā dhāvatyā ghoḍyācyā śilpāvara sthira basalele [...] āṇi tyā śilpācyā pāvalāṃkhāḷūna vāryācā ghoṃghoṃ āvāja karata jaga vegāne māgemāge jāta hota (*Te Don Manore*, 275)

> As Pippin was falling asleep, he had an unusual feeling. As if he and Gandalf were seated unmoving on a statue of a running horse [...] and beneath the footsteps of that statue, with the roaring noise of the wind, the world kept falling back rapidly (provisional translation, mine)[21]

> To tejasvī ghoḍā āṇi tyācyāvara basalelā to taruṇa Yayāti, doghehī unmatta hote. Doghehī kevala halate putale hote. Eka ghoḍyācā, dusarā māṇasācā. Ekā putalyāvara dusarā putalā basalelā! He donhī putale vilakṣaṇa vegāne dhāvata hote. (Khandekar 2017, 34)

> That radiant horse and that young Yayāti seated upon him, both were enthralled. Both were mere moving statues. One of the horse, the other of the man. One statue upon which was seated another! Both these statues were running at an incredible speed. (Provisional translation, mine)

While descriptions of nature also abound in this work, they are made to function as windows into the psychological states

21. The corresponding lines in Tolkien are “As he fell slowly into sleep, Pippin had a strange feeling: he and Gandalf were still as stone, seated upon the statue of a running horse, while the world rolled away beneath his feet with a great noise of wind” (*TT*, ‘The Palantír’, 600).

and worldviews of its three narrators thereby marking it as a psychological novel as well. Unlike Tolkien, Khandekar intended his work to be an allegorical social critique of the Indian man and society during the early 1950s in the aftermath of both World War II and the Indian independence movement (2017, 428-9, 441-52).

4 - Curious and Curiouser Cultural Evocations

The Marathi translation's word choices also contain the possibility of evoking some very curious - and at times, even jarring - cultural resonances. The translation of the words 'dark' and 'black' as *kṛṣṇa* in connection with Sauron and Mordor is a case in point. While *kṛṣṇa* is indeed a Sanskrit loanword meaning 'dark' and 'black', it is more commonly known as the name of a popular deity in Hindu religion (i.e., Krishna) and as such has the added connotative sense of 'beautiful' or 'attractive'. Thus, its use - often in conjunction with other words of Sanskrit derivation - brings about a jarring effect for those readers who associate these positive senses with the word and/or are the adherents of this religion.

This jarring effect can be best experienced through the translation of the 'Black' or 'Dark Land' as *kṛṣṇabhūmī*, the 'Shadow' as *kṛṣṇāchāyā*, the 'Black Gate' as *kṛṣṇādvāra*, the 'Lord of the Black Land' as *kṛṣṇabhūmīcā svāmī*, and the 'Dark Lord' as *kṛṣṇasvāmī*[22] and *kṛṣṇaśaktīcā svāmī*. The latter, which means 'lord of dark powers' or 'of the dark arts', alludes to more esoteric religious, occult practices and worldviews as well as superstitious beliefs. The Sanskrit loanword *dvāra* (door, gate) in connection with *kṛṣṇā* also evokes the Hindu

22. This word can also be translated as 'Lord Krishna'.

deity, Krishna's mythological city of Dwarka and its associated temple, which remains a popular place of pilgrimage.

The possibility of any misunderstanding concerning the intended referent of the word *kṛṣṇā* is averted by the translation's recourse to the word *kāḷā* - a more commonly used, connotatively neutral synonym, of Prakrit derivation, for 'dark' and 'black': for example, *kāḷī sāvalī* for the 'Shadow'; *kāḷī bhūmī* and *kāḷā deśa* for the 'Dark Land' and 'Black Country', respectively; *kāḷā manorā* for the 'Dark Tower'; *kāḷā paṃjā* for the 'Black Hand'; *kāḷā senāpatī* for the 'Black Captain'; *kāḷā svāra* for the 'Black Rider'; and *kāḷā śrvāsa* for the 'Black Breath'. This word, however, is rarely used to refer to Sauron himself: for example, only one instance each can be found of *kāḷā svāmī* for "dark master," *kāḷyā* for Gollum's "the Black One," and *kāḷā durātmā* (wicked soul) in place of "the Dark Lord" (*TT*, 'The Voice of Saruman', 580; 'The Black Gate is Closed', 643; *RK*, 'The Steward and the King', 966; *Te Don Manore*, 246, 336; *Rajache Punaragaman*, 316). Only rarely is he also referred to as *duṣṭa*, which means 'cruel' or 'hateful', thereby coming close to connoting the sense of evil. *Kṛṣṇā*, on the other hand, is not used even once for referring to the Black Riders.

In addition to the Sanskrit loanword *dvāra* and the Prakrit derived *dāra*, 'gates' in general and fortified gates in particular (i.e., the Black Gate, the Great Gate, and Helm's Gate) are also referred to using the Persian loanword *daravājā*. While this word is commonly used for doors of smaller structures like houses, temples, and so on, it also forms a standard component of the names of the fortified main gates of the approximately two to three hundred historical forts in the state of Maharashtra. While only some of these forts were built during the time of the Maratha kingdom under its founder Shivaji,[23] they remain associated with him in the socio-cultural, political imagination of Maharashtra in which he functions almost as an Arthurian equivalent. These associations become more pronounced in the translated descriptions of Hornburg and Minas Tirith, particularly through words like *killā* (fortress), *bālekillā* (upper fort or citadel), *buruja* (tower or bastion), and *taṭabaṃdī* (rampart), all of which belong to the nomenclature of these historical forts.[24]

The Maratha kingdom and its continuing influence on the present-day socio-political culture of Maharashtra is also evoked through the *tutārī* (a metal wind instrument), which is used in place of the 'trumpet' in a line from Gimli's Song of Durin (*Mudrikeche Sathidar*, 451; *FR*, 'A Journey in the Dark', 316). This instrument, with its distinctive heraldic sound associated with Maratha rulers, is still ceremoniously played today in front of the fortified gates of some key forts during certain anniversaries and festivals. The *tutārī* was also used once as a signal of war and was made of animal horns (see Lalitha and Nandini, 2018). However, the translation refrains from using the *tutārī* in such contexts and instead evokes these associations through the *śiṃga* and *raṇaśiṃga* (horn, war horn) besides retaining the English 'trumpet' in at least one instance (*Rajache Punaragaman*, 9). The 'drum' in Tolkien's text is similarly replaced with the *ḍhola* (a type of drum) and *nagarā*

23. The Maratha kingdom was founded by Chhatrapati (royal title for sovereign ruler) Shivaji Bhonsle in 1674. He is a figure of legend- and myth-making proportions in the socio-political imagination of Maharashtra and, as such, has been a constitutive part of the state's culture. He is a widely appropriated figure across political and activist spectrums.

24. For helpful diagrams and more information on the different types, structures, and nomenclature of the forts in Maharashtra, see Abhijit Rajadhyaksha (2011).

(a kind of kettledrum). However, the translation also uses *bherī* and *raṇabherī* (a kind of drum, war drum), *duṃdubhi* and *raṇaduṃdubhi* (another kind of kettledrum, war kettledrum), and the *nagarā* in place of the 'trumpet' in Tolkien's text.

The 'cloak' in Tolkien's work is similarly replaced with six different garments, none of which serves as a fitting equivalent: these garments are *sadarā, koṭa, śāla, aṃgarakhā, jhagā,* and *burakhā*. The word *aṃgarakhā*, a type of upper body robe that is wrapped and secured with ties, is also used to translate the word 'shirt' (*sadarā*) as well as 'coat' (*koṭa*). The *burakhā* (burqa) is frequently used for describing cloaked characters - from the hobbits, Aragorn, and Gandalf to the Nazgûl - when they are shrouded in darkness or are hooded. The *jhagā*, which refers to an ankle-length, flared garment, appears where the context is concerned with the length and draping of the cloak. The *śāla* (shawl) is used when the context additionally emphasizes a sense of chillness in the environment and the cold weather.

Of the many examples offered by the Marathi translation of Tolkien's work, the notion most difficult to translate, in my view, has been that of 'precious'. When it comes to Gollum's frequent use of this word, the translation relies on variations of a common term of endearment for children and loved ones: *sonyā, sonulī,* and *sonū*.[25] However, when it comes to characters like Isildur and Frodo, the translation exclusively uses the word *anamola* (priceless, very valuable). Gollum, on the other hand, is also made to take recourse to compound-forms like *anamola sonulī* and *anamola sonule*. Unfortunately, these commonly used terms of endearment are unable to

25. The Marathi translation of *The Hobbit* takes recourse to the word *śrīmaṃta* (rich, wealthy). This term is also used as a title for, among others, rulers of the Maratha empire or confederacy, particularly for the Peshwas.

capture the obsessiveness caused by the One Ring and indicate its corrupting influence - senses that accompany the word 'precious' in Tolkien's work. The assignment of another word - that is, *anamola* - for Isildur and Frodo comes in the way of any pattern formation via repetition thereby creating an obstruction for the reader in recognizing this tell-tale indicator of the evil influence and possession of the One Ring. Any such association is further undermined when *sonyā* is also used as an endearment by Gandalf, Pippin, and Frodo for Gimli and Pippin, Merry, and Sam, respectively (*Te Don Manore*, 132, 266; *Rajache Punaragaman*, 162, 178, 246).

Considering the issues and examples discussed in this paper, it would not be farfetched to claim in conclusion that this translation would have fared much better in terms of its quality - if not its saleability - had the translator acknowledged the existence of and taken the work's philosophical, theological themes and underpinnings, particularly that of the problem of evil, a bit more seriously.

Bibliography

Apte, Vaman Shivram, *The Practical Sanskrit–English Dictionary*, (Poona: Shiralkar & Co., 1890).

Balkavi [T.B. Thombre], '*Phularāṇī*', in *Bālakavīṃcyā Nivaḍaka Kavitā*, ed. by N.D. Mahanor (Shrirampur, Maharashtra: Shabdalaya Prakashan, 2011), pp. 30-33.

Chanda-Vaz, Urmi, 'What's Marathi for Orc? Translating "Lord of the Rings"', *Scroll.in*, 25 August 2015, <http://scroll.in/article/750778/whats-marathi-for-orc-translating-lord-of-the-rings> [accessed 22 October 2021].

Chavan, Dilip, 'The Standardisation of Marathi: Grammar and Lexicography', in *Language Politics under Colonialism: Caste, Class and Language Pedagogy in Western India*, (Newcastle upon Tyne: Cambridge Scholars Publishing, 2013), pp. 136-186.

Chunodkar, Sonali, 'An Indian Academic's Adventures in her Quest for the Perilous Realm', online video recording, YouTube, 27 July 2021, <https://www.youtube.com/watch?v=gOHRWefIEyE> [accessed 22 October 2021].

Collier, Pieter, 'Interview with Nilesh Pashte and Meena Kinikar about *The Hobbit* in Marathi', *Tolkien Library*, 25 September 2011, <http://www.tolkienlibrary.com/press/1011-Interview-marathi-hobbit-publisher-translator.php> [accessed 22 October 2021].

Fimi, Dimitra, *Tolkien, Race, and Cultural History: From Fairies to Hobbits*, (Basingstoke: Palgrave Macmillan, 2010).

Ghosh, Anando, 'Prakrit Language and Literature: A Brief Introduction', *Sahapedia*, 26 August 2020, < https://www.sahapedia.org/prakrit-language-and-literature-brief-introduction> [accessed 31 October 2021].

Jaaware, Aniket, 'Two Sentences: A Speculation of Genre in Early Marathi Novels', in *Early Novels in India*, ed. by Meenakshi Mukherjee (New Delhi: Sahitya Akademi, 2002), pp. 73-80.

Joshi, Poorva, 'Frodo speaks Marathi, in this Indian translation of LOTR', *Hindustan Times*, 18 September 2015, <https://www.hindustantimes.com/books/frodo-speaks-marathi-in-this-indian-translation-of-lotr/story-YNgY1EpXuxz7JFbYoDDwoI.html> [accessed 22 October 2021].

Karnik, Mugdha, 'Anuvādakāce Manogata' [Translator's Thoughts or Introduction], in *Swami Mudrikancha: Mudrikeche Sathidar*, (Pune: Diamond Publications, 2015), pp. ix-xiv.
--- 'Anuvāda Karatānā' [While Translating], blog post, *Aisi Akshare*, 25 March 2016, <https://aisiakshare.com/node/4984> [accessed 22 October 2021].

Khandekar, V.S., *Yayāti*, (Pune: Mehta Publishing House, 2017).

Lalitha, M., and M. Nandini, 'The Tutari's Sound is a Signal', *The Hindu*, 12 April 2018, <https://www.thehindu.com/entertainment/music/the-tutaris-sound-is-a-signal/article23512041.ece> [accessed 26 October 2021].

Molesworth, J.T., *A Dictionary, Marathi and English*, 2nd edn (Bombay: Bombay Education Society Press, 1857) <https://dsal.uchicago.edu/dictionaries/molesworth/> [accessed 26 October 26 2021].

Qasemi, S.H., and *EIr*, 'Marathi Language, Persian Elements in', *Encyclopædia Iranica*, 16 May 2013, <https://iranicaonline.org/articles/marathi-language> [accessed 31 October 2021].

Rajadhyaksha, Abhijit, 'Forts of Maharashtra', *The History Files*, 28 May 2011, <https://www.historyfiles.co.uk/FeaturesFarEast/India_Modern_Forts01.htm> [accessed 26 October 2021].

Roychowdhury, Adrija, 'There are 600 Potentially Endangered Languages in India ... Each Dead Language Takes Away a Culture System', *The Indian Express*, 3 May 2020, <https://indianexpress.com/article/research/international-mother-language-day-2018-ganesh-devy-indian-languages-5072487/> [accessed 21 September 2021].

Sohoni, Pushkar, 'Marathi of a Single Type: The Demise of the Modi Script', *Modern Asian Studies*, 51.3 (2016), 662-685 <https://doi.org/10.1017/S0026749X15000542>

Tolkien, J.R.R., *The Lord of the Rings*, (London: HarperCollins, 2005).
--- *The Hobbit*, trans. by Meena Kinikar (Pune: Diamond Publications, 2011).
--- *Swami Mudrikancha: Mudrikeche Sathidar*, trans. by Mugdha Karnik (Pune: Diamond Publications, 2015).
--- *Swami Mudrikancha: Te Don Manore*, trans. by Mugdha Karnik (Pune: Diamond Publications, 2015).
--- *Swami Mudrikancha: Rajache Punaragaman*, trans. by Mugdha Karnik (Pune: Diamond Publications, 2015).

A bridge invisible: motif borrowing and dislocation in Soviet bloc illustrations for *The Lord of the Rings*

Joel Merriner

The Akallabêth, the fourth part of *The Silmarillion* (edited by Christopher Tolkien from his father's texts) tells the tale of the downfall of Númenor, and the subsequent changing of the world by Ilúvatar wherein Arda was made round and Valinor and Eressëa were "taken away and removed beyond the reach of Men for ever" (334). After this cataclysm a path remained open between the two realms accessible to the Elves who were able to navigate their ships across and perhaps to others. Tolkien writes:

"Therefore the loremasters of Men said that a Straight Road must still be, for those that were permitted to find it. And they taught that, while the new world fell away, the old road and the path of the memory of the West still went on, as it were a mighty bridge invisible that passed through the air of breath and of flight (which were now bent as the world were bent), and traversed Ilmen which flesh unaided cannot endure" (338).

To illustrate this concept in terms of a minimalist piece of graphics (Fig. 1.) within the conceit of Tolkien's secondary world, his literary sub-creation, there exists, among others, the two realms of Valinor and Middle-earth, ostensibly separate but linked for some via an invisible bridge known as the "Straight Road" (*Silmarillion*, 338).

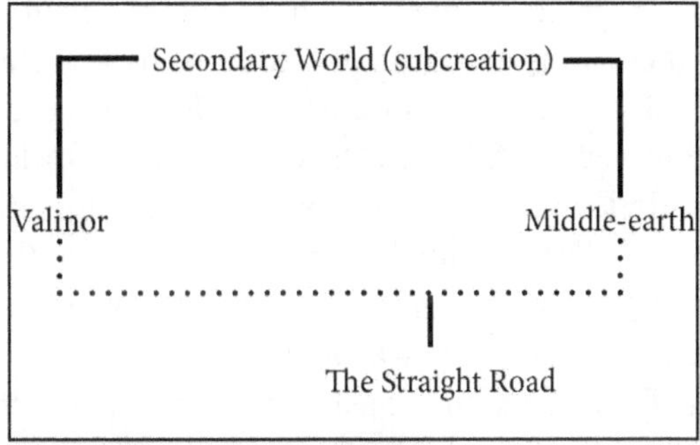

Fig. 1. Secondary world (sub-creation).

It is my belief that this concept provides a neat analogy of the path of visual interchange extant within Tolkien illustration (in this case Soviet Bloc Tolkien illustration) (Fig. 2.).

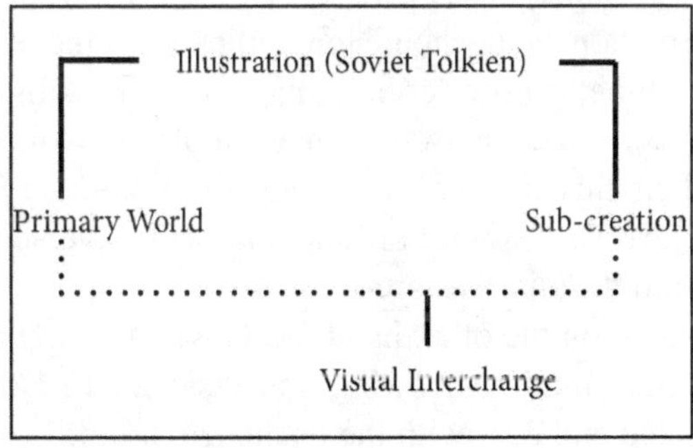

Fig. 2. Illustration (Soviet Tolkien).

In the place of Valinor we have the primary world, namely our world with its rich visual culture dating back millennia. Here exist millions of visual motifs waiting to be borrowed and incorporated into new works. In place of Middle-earth is

Tolkien's sub-creation, manifest here as Tolkien illustration. Between them runs the Straight Road equivalent, a "bridge invisible" (338), open to those artists able to access it, along which borrowed motifs may travel: primary world to sub-creation and vice versa, two realms influencing the other.

In *Hidden Visions*, my companion piece to this paper, presented at the *Tolkien and Diversity* seminar in July 2021,[1] I discussed how the Cold War-induced Otherness manifested in Soviet Bloc Tolkien translations remained particularly marked in 1980s illustrated editions of *The Lord of the Rings*. As touched upon in that paper, decoding the diverse, often cryptic illustrations contained within these books requires an interpretive approach tailored towards the understanding of three types of visual alterity identifiable in the region: motif borrowing, original creation and dislocation.

Hidden Visions dealt with the second form of alterity: original creation, a phenomenon typified by the enigmatic, often disturbing, censor defying imagery of the Polish Tolkien illustrator Jerzy Czerniawski; an example of which can be witnessed in this dust jacket image from Volume Three of *Władca Pierścieni*[2] wherein Frodo and Sam traverse the plain of Gorgoroth disguised as orcs.

This paper, on the other hand, deals with the first and third alterity forms: motif borrowing and dislocation. Both forms are connected and deal with the exchange of motifs, however, as we will see, dislocation is rooted in reception, how we as viewers perceive an image based on our own visual literacy

1. Published in Tolkien and Diversity (2023) The paper presentation can be seen here: https://www.youtube.com/watch?v=V3mNQ38tRRI.

2. Czerniawski's image can be viewed at minute 02:55 of the presentation recording: https://youtu.be/wPVqUY3Cdl0. All future references to the presentation recording in this article, will point to the cited link.

i.e., the pictures we already know and remember. An exemplar of this alterity form (to be discussed later in this paper) would be Èduard Zarjanskij's 1989 reimagining[3] of Tolkien's 1937 illustration *The Hill: Hobbiton-across-the Water*.[4]

I will begin my analysis by examining motif borrowing, which can be defined as the transferal of a visual motif (i.e., a theme, concept, idea, expressed by forms) from an earlier work into a new one. Here the artist effectively transfers visual material via the invisible bridge between the primary world of art history and Tolkien's sub-creation. Of course, this practice is not exclusively the preserve of Soviet Bloc artists but is a universal creative process. Within the specific field of Tolkien illustration, however, Tolkien himself makes frequent recourse to motif borrowing, accessing the bridge between two realms. These borrowings range from clear and obvious examples such as can be seen in the image *Glorund sets forth to seek Túrin* (1927)[5] which features a decorative border design derived from an Edward Johnston prototype[6] (itself based on an earlier medieval model) contained within instructional book *Writing & Illuminating & Lettering* (1906), to more generalised evocations of historical archetypes (Johnston 2006, 125). An example of the latter can be observed in the design of Lúthien Tinúviel's emblem[7] which bears a close resemblance

3. Zarjanskij's reimagining of Tolkien's image can be viewed at minute 16.21 of the presentation recording.

4. https://museoteca.com/r/en/work/7384/j_r_r_tolkien/the_hill_hobbiton_across_the_water/!/.

5. https://museoteca.com/r/en/work/7366/j_r_r_tolkien/glorund_sets_forth_to_seek_turin/!/

6. Johnston's prototype can be seen together with Tolkien's Glorund image at minute 4:447 of the presentation recording.

7. Tolkien's emblem for Lúthien Tinúviel can be viewed alongside a c. 15th century example of a "type A" consecration cross from Norfolk at minute 5:09 of the presentation recording.

to a form of post 15th century consecration cross classified by archaeologist John Henry Middleton as a "type A" cross (1885, 458).

Tolkien's sometime visual collaborator Pauline Baynes was also accustomed to motif borrowing, as evidenced by her image of a scribe (1949) from *Farmer Giles of Ham*[8] which recycles a motif from folio 323r *Reinmar von Zweiter*[9] of the c.1300 German illuminated manuscript *Codex Manesse* (Tolkien 2014, 54).

Motif borrowing then may not be unique to Soviet Bloc Tolkien artists, however the way in which they employ it often is. A typical example can be observed in the work of Győző Vida, illustrator of Adam Réz and Árpád Göncz's 1981 three volume Hungarian translation of *The Lord of the Rings* entitled *A Gyűrűk Ura*. Prior to his commissioning by the Budapest publishing house Gondolat, Vida had produced medieval-inspired images for Gáspár Soltész's 1979 Hungarian translation of Günter de Bruyn's *Tristan und Isolde*,[10] borrowing motifs directly from illuminated manuscript pages such as folio 69r *Herr Werner von Teufen of Codex Manesse.*[11]

Vida's contribution to the Hungarian Tolkien translation encompasses full colour dust jacket designs and a series of symbolic heraldic devices marking the opening of each of the six books. It is the dust jacket designs which exemplify Vida's motif borrowing; for example, his Volume One (*A Gyűrű*

8. Baynes' image can be seen at minute 5:20 of the presentation recording.
9. https://upload.wikimedia.org/wikipedia/commons/f/f0/Codex_Manesse_Reinmar_von_Zweter.jpg.
10. An example of Vida's images for Tristan und Isolde can be seen at minute 6:04 of the presentation recording.
11. https://upload.wikimedia.org/wikipedia/commons/5/55/Codex_Manesse_069r_Werner_von_Teufen.jpg.

Szövetsége) cover design,[12] which is clearly intended to depict the Argonath. The composition and colour scheme of this image are evocative of Pauline Baynes' Argonath vignette featured in the famous George Allen & Unwin *A Map of Middle-earth*[13] painted in 1969. Vida had a degree of familiarity with this map (a copy of which he may have obtained from the translation publishers Gondolat) and drew upon it for several images. Here for example, his dust jacket design for the back panel of Volume Three[14] recycles Baynes' twin-sailed Corsair craft from the Bay of Belfalas section of the map[15] to create the Last Ship bearing the Ringbearer's from the Grey Havens along the Straight Road.

Returning to the Argonath image, the lions at the feet of the two kings are distinctly uncanonical, and possibly constitute a borrowing from a primary world source, namely the tradition within medieval art of placing lions as symbolic footrests on the tomb effigies of famous knights. As confirmed by Tummers, the lion in this context can be seen as a symbol of the kingly state and of Resurrection, the latter being derived from the legend in which a lioness roars her still born cubs back to life (1980, 41-2). A related motif, of which Budapest-resident Vida would have been aware, can be observed in Kálmán Lux's 1930 sculpture depicting King Matthias I or Matthias Corvinus, the "Raven King" of Hungarian fame seated with his feet on a lion at the Bauthzen Matthias Memorial.[16] The presence of the lions

12. Vida's image can be seen at minute 6:24 of the presentation recording.
13. https://museoteca.com/r/en/work/7469/pauline_baynes/a_map_of_middle_earth/!/.
14. This image can be seen at minute 6:52 of the presentation recording.
15. A close up of Baynes' craft can be seen at minute 7:00 of the presentation recording.
16. https://upload.wikimedia.org/wikipedia/commons/4/42/Bautzen%2C_Ortenburg%2C_Matthias_Corvinus_of_Hungary_3024.JPG.

in Vida's Argonath are a symbol for the eternal power of Isildur and Anárion, many ages dead but, like Matthias, revered and effectively resurrected in statue form.

As a visual addendum, the grimaces and manes of Vida's lions correlate with the features of the two statues of lions holding shields on the staircase of the Neo-Romanesque Fisherman's Bastion[17] (built between 1895-1902), also in Budapest. The lions' shields on the Bastion coincidentally offer a solution to the uncanonical shields in Vida's image. Overall, this juxtaposing of primary world and Tolkienian motifs invites the viewer to draw parallels between the visual culture of medieval Europe (particularly Hungary) and Gondor.

A similar sentiment can be detected in the motif borrowing featured in Vida's image for the front panel of the dust jacket to Volume Three (*A Király Visszatér*).[18] Here we see a plate-armoured, moustachioed Aragorn sat astride a grey war horse. The image does not depict a specific narrative scene but instead broadly evokes the concept of a heroic individual returned to unite a fractured kingdom. Vida makes this more potent for his Hungarian audience by basing Aragorn's warhorse and his Verdigris-coloured armour directly on János Fadrusz's late 19th century bronze equestrian statue of Matthias I.[19] The popular perception of Matthias as a strong military leader, Renaissance ruler and a rebuilder of the Hungarian state resonates with Tolkien's notion of Aragorn as High King of a united Arnor and Gondor, leading his people into a new age of prosperity.

---

17. An example of one of these lions can be seen together with a close-up of Vida's Argonath at minute 8:19 of the presentation recording.
18. Vida's image can be seen at minute 9:00 of the presentation recording.
19. A close-up of Fadrusz's statue can be seen alongside Vida's Aragorn at minute 19:33 of the presentation recording.

The next example of motif borrowing concerns the Bulgarian artist Yasen Panov. Panov's illustrations for Lyubomir Nikolov's two volume 1990-1991 Bulgarian translation of *The Lord of the Rings*, entitled *Vlastelinat Na Prastenite* blend decorative and figurative modes to create a darkly archaic aesthetic. Panov emphasises narrative associations in his depictions, however his iconographical connections are primarily reserved for aspects of material culture (e.g., weapons, armour, architecture) and figures. His stark monochrome images have a distinctly Bulgarian flavour that is redolent of both Orthodox woodcut designs from the village of Samokov, and later, 20th century revivalist pieces by artists such as Vassil Zahariev.[20]

Aside from such potential regional influences, during the creation of his Tolkien illustrations Panov appears to have had access to several examples of Western Tolkien illustration, attested to by the motif borrowing present in his two highly striking dust jacket images.[21] Both designs follow the same compositional form, depicting groups of figures (on the back panel) stood before sinister fortresses which are closely modelled on Roger Garland's 1982 oil painting *Barad-dûr*;[22] an image originally featured on the cover of Unwin's 1983 single-volume paperback edition of *The Lord of the Rings* and in *The J.R.R. Tolkien Calendar 1984*.

Although Panov's illustrations are not identical to Garland's, numerous elements have been reproduced including the

20. An example of Vida's imagery can be seen alongside a Bulgarian Orthodox woodcut by Georgi Klinkov at minute 10:37 of the presentation recording.
21. The front panels of Vida's two dust jacket images can be seen at minute 10:55 of the presentation recording.
22. A cropped version of Garland's image can be seen at: https://www.theonering.com/barad-dur-roger-garland/.

pyramidic shape rising straight from the rocky crag, the path and bridge and the dramatic storm clouds forming a maelstrom above the highest tower. Why Panov has done this is open to conjecture, however for a neophyte Tolkien illustrator, borrowing motifs from an established artist (i.e., Garland) with a proven record of publications could be regarded as an easy way to invest his own work with a readymade air of Tolkienian visual authenticity.

Despite the obvious borrowed elements, Panov's structures have an ambiguity which makes attribution difficult. Identification relies primarily on their respective assemblages of figures. Volume One depicts Gandalf and Pippin on Shadowfax, a leopard skin clad Legolas (which is a new look for the Elf) and a suitably Dwarven Gimli.[23] Volume Two has a Nazgûl and two armoured Orcs plus a bearded man of the East.[24] This implies readings where the Volume One tower represents members of the Fellowship before Minas Morgul or Barad-dûr (it scarcely matters which). Volume Two has the servants of Sauron before Minas Tirith.

The apotheosis of motif borrowing within a Tolkienian visual context can be attributed to the Ukrainian artist Sergei Iukhimov, responsible for the illustrations in Izdatel's 1993 two volume edition of Natalya Grigor'eva and Vladimir Grushetskij's *Vlastelin Kolets* translation. Iukhimov's mosaic-like compositions fuse Insular illumination, hagiographic paintings, Antique solar imagery and Noldorin heraldry to create unique, hybrid Tolkienian forms.[25]

23. Both assemblages of figures occur on the back panels of their respective dust jackets. Volume One can be seen at minute 11:08 of the presentation recording.

24. This image can be seen at minute 11:12 of the presentation recording.

25. Examples of Iukhimov's mosaic-like compositions can be seen in minutes

Iukhimov uses motif borrowing in his imagery to both impart a flavour of the original work and to enhance and alter meaning within the new. In his *Pyre of Denethor* (1989)[26] he subverts Tolkien's canonical "heathen" suicide figure of Denethor by presenting a Steward of Gondor in the guise of the 2nd century Christian martyr Polycarp of Smyrna[27] (*RK*, 'The Siege of Gondor', 825). In a colour scheme echoing the black and white vestments of Polycarp, Denethor stands transfixed by a seven-crossed halo of power emanating from the palantír in his hands whilst simultaneously burning righteously like the martyr Anastasia of Sirmium in Tzortzis the Cretan's 17th century fresco from the *katholikon* of the Dionysiou monastery on Mt. Athos.[28] In combining the two martyrs (Polycarp and Anastasia) within the figure of Denethor Iukhimov has imbued his illustration with the ready-made philosophical and moral complexity of the Christian images whilst also injecting an element of irony.

I will conclude this paper by examining the third and most obscure form of visual alterity detectable in Soviet Bloc Tolkien illustration, a type of semiosis or signification process I refer to as dislocation. In its normal form, Tolkienian visual semiosis works as follows; take a hypothetical Soviet depiction of Aragorn wearing the crown of Gondor and imagine that the design of the crown is directly borrowed from Tolkien's own

---

13:05 to 13:17 of the presentation recording.

26. Iukhimov's image can be seen at minute 13:18 of the presentation recording.

27. Iukhimov's image can be seen alongside a close-up view of Polycarp featured in an anonymous 14th century fresco from the Visoki Dečani Monastery, Serbia at minute 13:42 of the presentation recording.

28. Tzortzis' depiction of Anastasia can be seen alongside Iukhimov's Denethor at minute 14:01 of the presentation recording.

original 1958 drawing.[29] The Soviet image of the crown is the signifier. It represents on paper the signified, that is Tolkien's textual description but also (if we are aware of the original drawing) the mental picture of Tolkien's own crown sketch which we see in our mind when we open the hypothetical Soviet book and look at the crown illustration. The signifier here is therefore stitched to its signified in a stable manner. The Soviet crown may differ slightly from Tolkien's but to the viewer it still signifies the crown of Gondor.

A variation of this is identifiable in Iukhimov's 1988 image *Sauron Defeated*, which when inverted[30] can be seen to be derived from the John the Evangelist miniature (folio 291v)[31] in the 9th century *Book of Kells*. Here Iukhimov's image can move between signifieds. It can travel freely back and forth across the invisible bridge between primary world and sub-creation – stably representing both the borrowed *Book of Kells* element and the Tolkienian figure of Sauron.

Dislocation, however, can be defined as the disturbance of a visual signifier from its usual signifier/signified context and function. In the corpus of Soviet Bloc Tolkien illustrations, the embodiment of this alterity form would be Èduard Zarjanskij's recreation of *The Hill: Hobbiton-across-the Water*, featured in *Khraniteli* ("Guardians"), Raduga's revised and unabridged 1989 version of Andrej Kistyakovskij and Vladimir Murav'ev's 1982 translation of *The Fellowship of the Ring*.[32]

29. https://tolkiengateway.net/w/images/b/b8/J.R.R._Tolkien_-_Crown_of_Gondor.svg.

30. This inverted version of Iukhimov's image can be seen together with Book of Kells Folio 291v at minute 15:32 of the presentation recording.

31. https://digitalcollections.tcd.ie/concern/folios/zg64tm24j?locale=en.

32. The 1989 Raduga edition of *Khraniteli* formed Volume One of a full translation of the trilogy, with Volumes Two (*Dve Tverdyni*) and Three (*Vozvrashen'e Gosudarya*) published in 1990 and 1992 respectively.

Zarjanskij's image is founded upon visual borrowing. When first opening the book and viewing the picture many viewers will experience a moment of recognition.[33] That sensation is the signifier/signified relationship working as it should. For a moment our mind accepts Zarjanskij's image as actually being Tolkien's. In this sense, and at this juncture, it functions as the signifier stitched to the signified notion of The Hill: Hobbiton-across-the-Water. It visually represents the landscape's conceptual likeness in precisely the same way as Tolkien's own image does. But it is only a fleeting experience, and that recognition quickly gives way to rejection, as the viewer becomes aware of the discrepancies in Zarjanskij's image.[34] This rejection is the signifier/signified relationship breaking down. Everything appears wrong about Zarjanskij's landscape. The road has become a river with a steamboat, the Hill is bare, the Hobbit-holes are gone, the topography is completely askew. To return to our minimalist graphic, Zarjanskij's landscape inhabits a strange dislocation netherworld between the primary world and secondary worlds, depicting neither a real place nor a Tolkienian one. As a disturbing postscript this entire process has the capacity to reoccur on subsequent viewings, with the viewer (dependent on their level of acquaintance with Tolkien's original image), progressing repeatedly from familiarity to rejection and then back again.

The four illustrators featured in this paper embody the practice of motif borrowing in a manner that is distinct to

---

Kistyakovskij died in 1987, leaving Murav'ev to translate the latter volumes alone. Like *Khraniteli*, the two new volumes were translated in unabridged form, save for the omission of the Volume Three Appendices.

33. Zarjanskij's image of The Hill can be seen in the context of the book itself in minutes 16:28 to 16:33 of the presentation recording.

34. Zarjanskij's and Tolkien's images can be seen together at minute 17:08 of of the presentation recording.

Soviet Bloc Tolkien. Győző Vida draws upon the illustrations of Pauline Baynes and the memorialising imagery of the Raven King Matthias Corvinus to create hybrid symbols of Hungarian and Gondorian glory; Yasen Panov channels the work of Roger Garland to forge ambiguous Middle-earth fortresses steeped in Tolkienian visual authenticity; Sergei Iukhimov brings the iconography of the Christian martyr to the Pyre of Denethor in a manner that subverts Tolkien's Steward of Gondor and Èduard Zarjanskij subsumes Tolkien's bucolic image of the Shire into a dislocated scene that hovers between primary and secondary worlds. The socio-political contexts in which these individuals operated were often difficult and restrictive, with access to visual material regularly policed by the censor. Nevertheless, just as Tolkien's Straight Road existed for those ships able, by grace of the Valar, to navigate its course, so another path of motif interchange remained open for those Soviet Bloc illustrators resourceful or lucky enough to access it: a bridge invisible, if you will, between the primary and Tolkienian visual worlds.

Bibliography

Garland, Roger, *The J.R.R Tolkien Calendar 1984*, (London: Unwin Paperbacks, 1983).

Middleton, John Henry, 'On Consecration Crosses, with Some English Examples', *Archaeologia*, 48 (1885), 456-464.

Tolkien, J.R.R., *Farmer Giles of Ham*, (London: HarperCollins, 2014).
--- *The Fellowship of the Ring*, (A Gyűrű Szövetsége), trans. by Ádám Réz and Árpád Göncz, (Budapest: Gondolat, 1981).
--- *The Fellowship of the Ring*, (Khraniteli), trans. by Andrej Kistyakovskij and Vladimir Murav'ev, (Moscow: Raduga, 1989).
--- *The Fellowship of the Ring*, (Wyprawa), trans. by Maria Skibniewska, (Warsaw: Czytelnik, 1981)
--- *The Lord of the Rings*, 3rd One Volume Edition, (London: Unwin Paperbacks, 1983).
--- *The Lord of the Rings*, (Vlastelin Kolets) Volume One, trans. by Natalya Grigor'eva and Vladimir Grushetskij, (Moscow: TO Izdatel', 1993).
--- *The Lord of the Rings*. (Vlastelin Kolets) Volume Two, trans. by Natalya Grigor'eva and Vladimir Grushetskij, (Moscow: TO Izdatel', 1993).
--- *The Lord of the Rings*. (Vlastelinat Na Prastenite) Volume One, trans. by Lyubomir Nikolov, (Sofia: Narodna Kultura, 1990).
--- *The Lord of the Rings*. (Vlastelinat Na Prastenite) Volume Two, trans. by Lyubomir Nikolov, (Sofia: Narodna Kultura, 1991).
--- *The Return of the King*. (A Király Visszatér), trans. by Ádám Réz and Árpád Göncz, (Budapest: Gondolat, 1981).
--- *The Return of the King*. (Powrót króla), trans. by Maria Skibniewska, (Warsaw: Czytelnik, 1981).
--- *The Silmarillion*, ed. by Christopher Tolkien, (London: HarperCollins, 2013).

Tummers, H. A., *Early Secular Effigies in England: The Thirteenth Century*, (Leiden: E.J. Brill, 1980).

From rabbits to Hobbits: illustrating and translating J.R.R. and Christopher Tolkien in France

Marie Bretagnolle

Since the first translation of *The Hobbit* in French in 1969, J.R.R. and Christopher Tolkien's texts have known different incarnations in the French publishing world, and many of them have included different ways of considering illustrations and maps.

J.R.R. Tolkien had a rather belated reception in France, starting in 1969 with the first French translation of *The Hobbit*. Even though he had little connection with France, the following study will show how his and his son's works were received successfully through the prism of translation and illustration.

This study will focus on the instances in which questions of translation meet questions of illustration and map-making, in order to see how one can influence the other, on purpose or not.

1 - The road of translation goes ever on

The very first unofficial translation into French of a piece by J.R.R. Tolkien was in 1937, when Simonne d'Ardenne, one of J.R.R. Tolkien's students and a specialist of Middle-English, worked privately on *Farmer Giles of Ham*.[1] The author was interested in the process of translation and was satisfied with

1. The chronology of the first translation projects is available in Wayne G. Hammond and Christina Scull's *The J.R.R. Tolkien Companion and Guide*, 3 v., London, HarperCollinsPublishers, 2017.

her work, so much so that he suggested her name for future translations.

A French translation of *The Hobbit* was discussed as early as 1937 (Hammond and Scull 2017, vol. 1, 329) and again around 1956, but for many different reasons it was only published in 1969, not with Simonne d'Ardenne but with Francis Ledoux. He had previously worked on Charles Dickens, Herman Melville, Edgar Allan Poe, William Shakespeare and Charlotte Brontë, to name a few. In 1969, Ledoux did not have access to most of the material that was published from 1977 onwards. From the very first translation of J.R.R. Tolkien into French, lasting mistakes were made. Some were due to this lack of information, when others were simply typographical errors.

In the first French translation of *The Lord of the Rings* published in France between 1972 and 1973, there were no author's foreword, no appendices, and no index. The only exception was the 'Tale of Aragorn and Arwen' which seems to have had Francis Ledoux's favour. The rest of the appendices and the index were translated 13 years later, in 1986, by Tina Jolas, in a four-volume edition of *The Lord of the Rings* published by Christian Bourgois (Ferré 2014).

Francis Ledoux's translation of *The Lord of the Rings* did not always follow J.R.R. Tolkien's instructions to translators, nor did it follow Ledoux's previous work on *The Hobbit* in which he had left most of the names in their original form. In the 1969 French *Hobbit*, we follow the adventures of Bilbo Baggins, with his original name, but when the first chapter of *The Lord of the Rings* in French opens, we are at Bilbon Sacquet's birthday party.

One of the most remarkable misconceptions in *The Lord of the Rings* appears in the prologue, where we read: "bien qu'Elrond fût mort" (*La Communauté de l'Anneau*, livre 1,

"Note sur les archives de la Comté", 42), which means "though Elrond had died" instead of "though Elrond had departed" as it reads in the original text (*FR*, 'Prologue', 28). Faced with the word "departed/departure", used in the chapter 'The Departure of Boromir', Ledoux did not have *The Silmarillion* to know that Elrond (as well as Galadriel) had sailed to the Undying Lands rather than died.

Fortunately, Ledoux's work also had his qualities, and it stayed in the collective imagination as the version used in the French version of Peter Jackson's movie trilogies.

When *The Silmarillion* came out in 1977, the French publisher Christian Bourgois was determined to have a French version available as soon as possible. He contacted Pierre Alien, a translator he had worked with before. Unfortunately Alien hated the book. His translation included errors and even missed a few lines. He was not familiar with the legendarium and did not have access to the wealth of information published from 1980 onwards by Christopher Tolkien, which led, again, to misunderstandings.

Patient French fans collected errata in online forums for years, regarding *The Silmarillion* as well as *The Hobbit* and *The Lord of the Rings*. They paved the way for a new translation. It was undertaken by the Canadian translator Daniel Lauzon, who took an active part in fan forums hunting down translation errors. His first published contribution was a collaboration (with Elen Riot) on *The Lays of Beleriand* in 2006, after which he translated *The Shaping of Middle-earth* (2007) and *The Lost Road and Other Writings* (2008). His new translation of *The Hobbit* was partly motivated by the French edition of *The Annotated Hobbit* in 2012 as well as the 75th anniversary of the publication of *The Hobbit*. Such a close study of the text as Douglas Anderson did, demanded that the French version be revised in order to be as close to J.R.R. Tolkien's narrative and style as possible.

Afterwards, Lauzon prepared a new translation of *The Lord of the Rings*, published between 2014 and 2016, and in 2021 he released the new translation of *The Silmarillion* in an edition featuring Ted Nasmith's new illustrations. By 2021, Daniel Lauzon had been working on J.R.R. and Christopher Tolkien's works for 15 years. Before him, translations had been conducted by seven different translators in eleven years. The past dozen years have seen a harmony being reached regarding Tolkien in translation in France. This endeavour has also deeply benefitted from the dedication of Adam Tolkien, Christopher's son, who translated several of his father and grandfather's texts, including *The Book of Lost Tales*, and worked on the Tolkien Estate's website.

2 - Unique books in the French corpus: *Faërie* and *Etymologies*

Despite the small size of Christian Bourgois éditeur, the publishing house owning Tolkien's translation rights in France are dedicated to giving as much access to J.R.R. Tolkien's and Christopher Tolkien's writings as possible to the French readership. This interest, blending fan and academic perspective respectively, has led to two publications which are specific to France.

Christian Bourgois published in 1974 the volume *Faërie*, which was prompted by the 1964 publication of *Tree and Leaf*. However, *Faërie* does not only contain 'On Fairy-stories' and 'Leaf by Niggle', 'Farmer Giles of Ham' and 'Smith of Wootton Major' also appear in the volume. This book brought together texts which had been published separately. In English, they were gathered in the volume *Poems and Stories* in 1980.

The second book in our focus here is not a collection of separate texts, but the edition of a chapter from *The History of Middle-earth* in a single volume. In October 2009, Christian Bourgois editions published a unique book entitled *Etymologies*. It was not prompted by a publication from HarperCollins. It did not and still does not have a direct equivalent in English as a single volume. 'Etymologies' is a chapter taken from *The Lost Road*, volume 5 in *The History of Middle-earth*, published in 1987.

This section is an etymological dictionary of a hundred pages or so, providing a deep dive into J.R.R. Tolkien's language creation. Ever since its publication in English, some corrections had been noted by Christopher Tolkien and the editors of the journal *Vinyar Tengwar*, Carl Hostetter and Patrick H. Wynne. When the time came to translate *The Lost Road* into French, in 2008, Vincent Ferré, Tolkien scholar and director of collection for Christian Bourgois, Daniel Lauzon, the translator, and the publisher at Christian Bourgois asked Christopher Tolkien and the Tolkien Estate if it was possible to take into consideration the corrections published in *Vinyar Tengwar*. This raised several issues, because it would go beyond an already complex translation process to publish *The Lost Road* in France. It was finally agreed that *The Lost Road* would be left intact, so as to keep a trace of the volume as it was published in the 1980s. However, a separate edition of this chapter on etymologies felt like the right place to highlight those adjustments made by scholars and specialists.

Etymologies was published in 2009, a year after the French translation of *The Lost Road*. It appears in a small companion volume with a cover and interior illustrations taken from Alan Lee's work on *The Children of Húrin*.

These two examples show how the French publishers are determined to work towards the recognition of J.R.R. and Christopher Tolkien's works in France, while also working within the limits of their scale. Christian Bourgois éditeur is not as large a publishing company as HarperCollins, so they cannot provide translations of each and every book that comes out in English. This is why there is no volume equivalent to *Tales from the Perilous Realm*, for instance, which brought together texts published elsewhere, for instance in *Faërie*. Although many texts by J.R.R. and Christopher Tolkien remain to be translated, starting with volumes 6 to 12 of *The History of Middle-earth*, the French publishers continue the work of sharing their work with the French readership. For instance, they have responded quickly to the publication of the Three Great Tales: *The Children of Húrin*, *Beren and Lúthien* and *The Fall of Gondolin* as illustrated by Alan Lee.

3 - Mapping French translations

Before turning to the question of illustration, the first area in which translation and pictures meet in J.R.R. and Christopher Tolkien's books is the maps.

In the first French editions of *The Hobbit*, the handwritten names on the maps in English were replaced with typography. Most of them were translated, with the exception of the name "Mirkwood". An especially curious and lasting mistake was made in the "Map of Wilderland": it features an arrow in the bottom left-hand corner, pointing in the direction of Hobbiton. In French, there was a confusion between Hobbits and rabbits, which led the arrow to point in the direction of "les lapins" ("rabbits").

The association of hobbits and rabbits had previously been encouraged on a strictly phonetic basis by the French publisher, who had suggested translating "Hobbits" by "Hopins". Tolkien did not object, underlining the fact that "Hopin" bore a resemblance to the word "lapin", French for "rabbit" which was itself close to "Hobbit". Tolkien did add in the same letter that he had never intended that connection, and he warned illustrators against the idea of creating a similar association in pictures: "as long as any illustrator is aware that this should not influence him unduly" (Hammond and Scull 2017, vol. 3, 451).[2] In the 1969 translation, the word "Hobbit" was kept, but "Hobbiton" was mistakenly read as "Rabbits" and so in French editions of *The Hobbit* the "Map of Wilderland" has indicated the direction of rabbits until 2010 when the mistake was corrected.

In the first illustrated French translation of *The Lord of the Rings*, in 1978, the maps of Middle-earth are not translated.[3] They are reproduced as they appear in the English editions, and this is not the only part that is missing in the translation, as we saw earlier. This may have created some confusion in the readers, as for instance they can spot the Dead Marshes on the map but their French name (Marais des Morts) is not given. As for the Map of the Shire in the same volume, it was partly translated: most of the place names are given in French, but some are left in the original language. The map of the Shire thus shows mostly French-looking words, with a few exceptions such as "Oatbarton" or "Rushock". It seems

2. Letter dated from 15 May 1968, quoted from the Tolkien-George Allen & Unwin archive at HarperCollins).
3. Pictures are available on Tolkiendil's website: https://www.tolkiendil.com/tolkien/biblio/sda/editions_reliees_ledoux (accessed 25 October 2021).

to concern mainly names that are not mentioned in the text, although further research would be necessary here.

Ten years later, in the edition of *The Lord of the Rings* illustrated by Philippe Munch and published in 1988, the artist redrew the map of Middle-earth and the map of the Shire. This time, the map showing "The West of Middle-earth at the End of the Third Age" was fully translated. It appears twice in the book: the first time between the title page and the Ring verse, and the second time next to the map of the Shire before chapter one. What is surprising is that the two maps of Middle-earth are redrawn versions of Christopher Tolkien's version, with French names, but they are different from each other. The first one, covering a double page, has shading and grey tones and shows the entirety of the map, whereas the second one is cut at the latitude of Fangorn Forest. The names are also placed in slightly different positions. The map base seems to be the same, the difference in shading being due to reproduction techniques, but there remains the question of why the names were handwritten twice.

In the new translated editions of *The Lord of the Rings*, published between 2014 and 2016, and in the new translation of *The Silmarillion*, published in October 2021, Daniel Lauzon translated every translatable word on the maps and made sure to preserve their aesthetic as well. In order to keep Christopher Tolkien's penmanship, the translator became a graphic designer and reused Christopher Tolkien's calligraphy to turn English words into French. He shared on his Twitter account a video clip of his process. The result is a seamless map that seems to have been penned directly in French, which creates a very harmonious edition.

4 - Specificities of French illustrations

This search of harmony also guided the editorial choices made by the French publisher in the past twenty years. Before that, four illustrated editions were published between 1976 and 1988: two *Hobbits* and two *Lord of the Rings*. Most of them are in black and white with chapter headings, but the 1976 *Hobbit* also features full-page colour illustrations, showing mainly the characters and snippets of their environment.

This edition, illustrated by French artist Chica, features on its cover a very happy-looking and childish Bilbo, making his way in a sort of jungle in tones of yellow, orange and green. The illustrations inside the book are perhaps closest to those of António Quadros for the 1962 Portuguese edition, in which Bilbo also appeared very childish, which J.R.R. Tolkien hated. They do make interesting choices, as in the picture of Bilbo escaping from the Misty Mountains, in which he is shown directly from above, standing in the doorway while a half-circle of goblins are waiting to capture him. Under Chica's pen, Gollum is a cousin of the Creature from the Black Lagoon, but his attitude is not particularly frightening. Chica's illustrations often show characters in pairs: Bilbo and Gandalf, Bilbo and Gollum, Bilbo and a Dwarf emerging from a barrel, etc. It creates a mirror effect when the book opens on a full-page, black-and-white illustration of Bilbo and Gandalf on foot and closes with a very similar picture of the two of them on horse- and pony-back. In the two drawings, Bilbo has the exact same expression, as if the adventures he had lived had been of little importance.

In Evelyne Drouhin's 1983 illustrated *Hobbit*, the same picture of the Hobbit sitting and smoking is repeated every couple of chapters. This is an equivalent to the literary device of making Bilbo tell his story, although it is not as clear in *The Hobbit* as it is in *The Lord of the Rings*, in which we learn about the Red Book. However, it serves as a visual indication to the reader that the main character is telling his own story. There are many other illustrations in black and white, most of them within the text rather than as chapter headings. A few are full page. With the exception of the repeated illustration of Bilbo, all of them are captioned with a line in italics. Some of these are quotes, but others are slightly rewritten to be as concise as possible. As a general rule, Evelyne Drouhin's illustrations feature mainly round and childish characters, and a very limited number of locations. Having a lot of characters and captions for each illustration makes this edition particularly suited to children. Although she does not shy away from the picture, the battle at the end, her vision is of a chaotic scene more than a violent one. As for Smaug, she gives only one illustration of the dragon (except for the cover), when he is still sleeping on his treasure. She uses the highlights and shadow very cleverly in this picture to show Bilbo wearing the Ring and stealing a cup: his legs are merely outlines against the white background, whereas his dark jacket mingles with the shadows cast by Smaug's huge figure. At first glance, the viewers barely see him although he is standing in the foreground.

For the 1988 French *Lord of the Rings*, Philippe Munch drew two pictures per chapter in a style reminiscent of comic books. His illustrations offer a variety of topics, from landscapes and cityscapes to character portraits and objects of interest. He draws with as much detail Aragorn's chainmail shirt and the mountain sides sheltering Helm's Deep. He is one of the rare artists not taking inspiration from Tolkien's iconic view of Rivendell for the chapter 'Many Meetings' (in which he draws Gandalf by Frodo's bedside, the two having a chat after the

Hobbit woke up), and not to model Meduseld on Anglo-Saxon architecture (it rather looks like a vision from the 1001 nights, with shining, bulbous domes towering above a maze of smaller habitations with flat roofs).

The covers of this 6-volume edition were not drawn by Philippe Munch but by Christian Broutin. Although the former followed the text quite closely, the latter's interpretations are slightly more distant. The first volume features a sharp-toothed and red-eyed creature with the shape of a hill and skin like a flower-sprinkled meadow. Book 3 has a dark silhouette, possibly a Black Rider, astride an animal which looks like a chicken from the neck down and a dinosaur from the neck up. As for Book 4, it features a Hobbit (with sensible kneepads) wielding a sword that shines such a bright red that it is closer to a light sabre.

From 1997 onwards, the French publishers have closely followed the English illustrated editions, which has led to a progressive disappearance of the French illustrations. In 2007, the illustrations by Philippe Munch for *The Lord of the Rings* were republished, but recent editions are either the Alan Lee editions in large format, or the paperbacks without illustrations. The same goes for *The Hobbit*: the illustrations by French artists can be found second-hand, but not as new editions.

The illustrated French corpus is now dominated by Alan Lee and Ted Nasmith, just as it is in English editions.

5 - Conclusion

Today, the story of the reception of J.R.R. and Christopher Tolkien in France continues with the upcoming translation of *Sauron Defeated*, volume 9 in *The History of Middle-earth* (to be published in 2023), but also with projects such as "Aubusson weaves Tolkien", celebrating the author's love for craftsmanship and his own talent for illustration. The whole project encompasses 13 wall tapestries and a carpet, reproducing pictures from the legendarium as well as the *Letters from Father Christmas*.

Although there has not been a Tolkien book illustrated by a French artist since 1988, the long history of translation and illustration before that, and the continued efforts to make his manuscripts available to the French readership, show the dedication of French fans and scholars to this very English author. In September 2022 Christian Bourgois éditeur republished *Etymologies* in a single volume, without Alan Lee's drawings from *The Children of Húrin* but with Tolkien's design for the Gate of Moria on the cover, highlighting once more the close relationship between translation and images in Tolkien's works.

Bibliography

Tolkien, J.R.R., *Bilbo le Hobbit*, translated by Francis Ledoux and illustrated by Chica, Paris, Bibliothèque Verte, 1976.
--- *Le Seigneur des Anneaux*, 3 v., translated by Francis Ledoux and illustrated by Jean-Pierre Evrard, Paris, Jean-Jacques Pauvert, 1978.
--- *Le Silmarillion*, translated by Pierre Alien, Paris, Christian Bourgois éditeur, 1978.
--- *Bilbo le Hobbit*, translated by Francis Ledoux and illustrated by Evelyne Drouhin, Paris, Le Livre de Poche Jeunesse, 1983.
--- *Le Seigneur des Anneaux*, 3 v., translated by Francis Ledoux and illustrated by Philippe Munch, Paris, Folio Junior, 1988.
--- *The Lord of the Rings*, illustrated by Alan Lee, London, HarperCollins, 1991.
--- *Le Hobbit*, translated by Daniel Lauzon and illustrated by Alan Lee, Paris, Christian Bourgois éditeur, 2012.
--- *Le Seigneur des Anneaux*, 3 v., translated by Daniel Lauzon and illustrated by Alan Lee, Paris, Christian Bourgois éditeur, 2014; 2015; 2016.
--- *Le Silmarillion*, translated by Daniel Lauzon and illustrated by Ted Nasmith, Paris, Christian Bourgois éditeur, 2021.

Hammond, Wayne G. and Christina Scull, *The J.R.R. Tolkien Companion & Guide*, 3 v., London, HarperCollinsPublishers, 2017.

Ferré, Vincent, *Tolkien, trente ans après* (1973- 2003), Paris, Christian Bourgois Editeur, 2004.
--- *Lire J.R.R. Tolkien*, Paris, Pocket, 2014.

Interview with Daniel Lauzon and Vincent Ferré for Tolkiendil, September 2012. URL: https://www.tolkiendil.com/tolkien/portraits/interviews/daniel_lauzon/2012_sept

Interview with Clément Ribes for Tolkiendil, November 2020. URL: https://www.tolkiendil.com/tolkien/interviews/clement_ribes_2020

Des lapins aux Hobbits : illustrer et traduire J.R.R. et Christopher Tolkien en France

Marie Bretagnolle

Depuis la première traduction du *Hobbit* en français en 1969, les textes de J.R.R. et Christopher Tolkien ont connu différentes incarnations dans le monde de l'édition français, et nombre d'entre elles ont inclus des regards variés sur les illustrations et les cartes.

J.R.R. Tolkien a connu une réception relativement tardive en France, à partir de 1969 avec la première traduction du *Hobbit*. Malgré le peu de relation avec la France que l'auteur entretenait, l'étude suivante se propose de montrer comment son travail et celui de son fils ont bénéficié d'une réception fructueuse à travers le prisme de la traduction et de l'illustration.

On étudiera ici les cas de rencontre entre les questions de traduction, d'illustration et de cartographie, afin d'examiner comment les unes peuvent influencer les autres, de manière volontaire ou non.

1 - La route de la traduction se poursuit sans fin

La toute première traduction non officielle en français d'un texte de J.R.R. Tolkien apparaît en 1937, quand Simone d'Ardenne, l'une des étudiantes de l'écrivain-professeur et une spécialiste de Moyen Anglais, travaille de manière privée sur *Farmer Giles of Ham*.[1] J.R.R. Tolkien s'est intéressé au

1. La chronologie des premiers projets de traduction est détaillée par Wayne

processus de traduction et a exprimé sa satisfaction face au travail de d'Ardenne, au point qu'il a suggéré son nom pour de futures traductions.

Une traduction française du *Hobbit* est en projet dès 1937 (Hammond & Scull 2017, vol. 1, 329) puis à nouveau vers 1956, mais pour beaucoup de raisons différentes elle n'aboutit qu'en 1969, dans la version de Francis Ledoux. Ce dernier avait travaillé auparavant sur les textes de Charles Dickens, Herman Melville, Edgar Allan Poe, William Shakespeare et Charlotte Brontë, pour ne citer que ces noms. A l'époque, Ledoux n'avait pas accès à la plupart des documents édités et publiés à partir de 1977. C'est ainsi que depuis la toute première traduction de J.R.R. Tolkien en français, des erreurs durables sont commises. Certaines sont dues à ce manque d'information, tandis que d'autres sont d'ordre typographique.

Dans la première traduction française du *Seigneur des Anneaux* par Francis Ledoux, publiée en France entre 1972 et 1973, il n'y avait ni avant-propos de l'auteur, ni appendices, ni index. La seule exception était le « fragment du conte d'Aragorn et Arwen » (Appendice A, I, v) qui avait apparemment la faveur de Ledoux. Le reste des appendices et l'index sont publiés 13 ans plus tard, en 1986, par Tina Jolas dans l'édition en quatre volumes du *Seigneur des Anneaux* publiée par Christian Bourgois (Ferré 2014).

La traduction par Ledoux du *Seigneur des Anneaux* ne suit pas toujours les instructions laissées par J.R.R. Tolkien aux futurs traducteurs et traductrices, ni même le propre travail de Ledoux sur *Bilbo le Hobbit*, dans lesquels il avait laissé la plupart des noms sous leur forme originelle. Dans le *Hobbit* de 1969, on suit les aventures de Bilbo Baggins, avec

G. Hammond and Christina Scull dans *The J.R.R. Tolkien Companion and Guide*, 3 v., Londres, HarperCollinsPublishers, 2017.

son nom anglais, mais quand le premier chapitre du *Seigneur des Anneaux* s'ouvre, le lectorat se trouve plongé dans la fête d'anniversaire de Bilbon Sacquet.

L'un des malentendus les plus notables dans *Le Seigneur des Anneaux* apparaît dans le prologue, où on lit « bien qu'Elrond fût mort » (*La Communauté de l'Anneau, livre 1*, "Note sur les archives de la Comté", 42) pour "though Elrond had departed" (*FR*, 'Prologue', 28). En rencontrant le mot « departed » / « departure », également utilisé dans le chapitre «The Departure of Boromir », Ledoux ne disposait pas du *Silmarillion* pour savoir qu'Elrond n'était pas mort mais avait pris le bateau vers les Terres Immortelles.

Heureusement, le travail de Ledoux a aussi ses qualités. Il est resté dans l'imaginaire collectif comme la traduction utilisée dans la version française des trilogies cinématographiques de Peter Jackson.

Quand *The Silmarillion* paraît en 1977, l'éditeur français Christian Bourgois est déterminé à publier une version française aussi vite que possible. Il contacte Pierre Alien, un traducteur avec lequel il avait déjà travaillé. Malheureusement, Alien détesta le livre ; sa traduction inclue des erreurs et passe même outre certaines phrases. Alien n'était pas familier du légendaire et n'avait pas non plus accès à toutes les informations rendues disponibles à partir de 1980 par Christopher Tolkien. Ce manque conduit, là aussi, à des malentendus.

De patients fans français ont rassemblé des errata dans des forums en ligne pendant des années, sur *Le Silmarillion* mais aussi *Bilbo le Hobbit* et *Le Seigneur des Anneaux*. Ils ont ainsi préparé le terrain pour une nouvelle traduction. Celle-ci est entreprise par le traducteur canadien Daniel Lauzon, qui a participé activement à ces mêmes forums qui traquaient les erreurs dans les versions françaises. Sa première contribution publiée est une collaboration avec Elen Riot aux *Lais du Beleriand* en 2006, après quoi il a traduit *La Formation de la Terre du Milieu* (2007) et *La Route Perdue* (2008). Sa nouvelle traduction du *Hobbit* est en partie motivée par l'édition française du *Hobbit annoté* en 2012 ainsi que le 75ème anniversaire de la publication du *Hobbit*. Une étude aussi poussée que celle de Douglas Anderson demande en effet que la version française soit au moins révisée pour s'approcher au plus près du récit et du style de J.R.R. Tolkien que possible. C'est le choix d'une traduction entièrement nouvelle qui est fait, ouvrant la voie à une série de publications.

Par la suite, Lauzon prépare une nouvelle traduction du *Seigneur des Anneaux*, publiée entre 2014 et 2016, et il vient d'achever une nouvelle traduction du *Silmarillion* (dans une édition incluant les nouvelles illustrations de Ted Nasmith). En 2021, cela fait quinze ans que Daniel Lauzon travaille sur les manuscrits de J.R.R. et Christopher Tolkien. Avant lui, les traductions avaient été menées par sept traducteurs et traductrices différent(e)s en onze ans. Ces dernières années ont ainsi vu une nouvelle harmonie dans la traduction de Tolkien père et fils en France. Cette entreprise a aussi profondément bénéficié du dévouement d'Adam Tolkien, le fils de Christopher Tolkien, qui a traduit plusieurs textes de son père et son grand-père, notamment *Le Livre des Contes Perdus*, et a travaillé au site internet du Tolkien Estate.

2 - Des livres uniques dans le corpus français : *Faërie* et *Etymologies*.

Malgré la petite taille de la maison d'édition Christian Bourgois, qui possède les droits de traduction pour les Tolkien en France, celle-ci est déterminée à donner accès aux textes des deux auteurs autant que possible. Cet intérêt, qui mêle les perspectives faniques et académiques, a donné lieu à deux publications spécifiques à la France.

En 1974, Christian Bourgois publie le volume *Faërie*, qui est motivé par la publication en 1964 de *Tree and Leaf*. Cependant, *Faërie* ne contient pas seulement « Du Conte de Fées » et « Feuille, de Niggle », comme le veut le sommaire de *Tree and Leaf* : « Le Fermier Gilles de Ham » et « Smith de Grand Wootton » apparaissent également dans le volume. Ce livre rassemble des textes qui avaient jusqu'ici été publiés séparément. En anglais, il ne sont publiés ensemble que dans *Poems and Stories* en 1980.

Le second livre en question ici n'est pas un recueil de textes issus de sources différentes, mais l'édition d'un chapitre de *L'Histoire de la Terre du Milieu* en un volume unique. En octobre 2009, les éditions Christian Bourgois publient un petit livre intitulé *Etymologies*. Il ne fait pas suite à une publication en anglais chez HarperCollins. Il n'avait alors, et n'a toujours pas aujourd'hui, d'équivalent direct en anglais dans un volume unique. « Etymologies » est un chapitre tiré de *La Route perdue*, le volume 5 de *L'Histoire de la Terre du Milieu*, publié en 1987.

Cette section est un dictionnaire étymologique d'une centaine de pages, qui offre une plongée dans la création de langues par J.R.R. Tolkien. Depuis la publication de *La Route Perdue*, des corrections avaient été relevées par Christopher Tolkien et les rédacteurs du journal *Vinyar Tengwar*, Carl Hostetter et Patrick H. Wynne. Quand le moment est venu de traduire *La Route perdue* en français, en 2008, Vincent Ferré, spécialiste de Tolkien et directeur de collection chez Christian Bourgois éditeur, ainsi que Daniel Lauzon, le traducteur, et la maison d'édition elle-même, ont demandé à Christopher Tolkien et au

Tolkien Estate (les ayants-droits de la famille Tolkien) s'il était possible de prendre en compte les corrections publiées dans *Vinyar Tengwar*. Cela a soulevé plusieurs questions, car cela aurait été plus loin qu'un processus de traduction déjà complexe pour publier *La Route perdue* en France. Il a finalement été décidé que *La Route perdue* serait inchangé, afin de garder une trace du volume tel qu'il est publié dans les années 1980. En revanche, une édition séparée de ce chapitre sur les étymologies devient le lieu de mettre en lumière les corrections apportées par des universitaires et des spécialistes.

Etymologies est publié en 2009, un an après la traduction de *La Route perdue*. Il prend la forme d'un petit volume avec une couverture et des illustrations intérieures tirées du travail d'Alan Lee pour *Les Enfants de Húrin*.

Ces deux exemples montrent combien la maison d'édition française travaille en vue de la reconnaissance de l'œuvre de J.R.R. et Christopher Tolkien en France, tout en opérant au sein de ses propres limites. Christian Bourgois éditeur n'est pas une maison d'une taille équivalente à HarperCollins, donc elle n'est pas en mesure de proposer des traductions de chaque livre qui sort en anglais par ou à propos de J.R.R. et Christopher Tolkien. C'est pour cette raison qu'il n'existe pas d'équivalent français à *Tales from the Perilous Realm*, par exemple, qui rassemble des textes publiés en France dans des volumes séparés, et notamment dans Faërie. Bien que de nombreux textes de Tolkien père et fils restent à traduire, à commencer par les volumes 6 à 12 de *L'Histoire de la Terre du Milieu*, Christian Bourgois éditeur poursuit ce travail de partage avec le lectorat français. Par exemple, il a répondu rapidement à la publication des trois grands contes : *Les Enfants de Húrin*, *Beren et Lúthien* et *La Chute de Gondolin*, tous les trois illustrés par Alan Lee.

3 - Cartographier les traductions françaises

Avant de poursuivre avec la question de l'illustration, le premier endroit où se rencontrent texte et image dans les livres de J.R.R. et Christopher Tolkien est la cartographie.

Dans les premières éditions françaises du *Hobbit*, les mots manuscrits sur les cartes en anglais sont remplacés par de la typographie. La plupart sont traduits, à l'exception du nom « Mirkwood ». Une erreur durable et particulièrement curieuse est faite dans la carte « Les Terres Sauvages » du *Hobbit* : on y trouve une flèche dans le coin inférieur gauche, pointant dans la direction de Hobbiteville. En français, une confusion entre « Hobbit » et l'anglais « rabbit » a conduit la flèche à pointer vers « les lapins ».

L'association entre Hobbits et lapins avait été encouragée auparavant sur une base strictement phonétique, quand l'éditeur français avait suggéré de traduire « Hobbits » par « Hopins ». J.R.R. Tolkien ne s'y était pas opposé, soulignant le fait que « Hopin » ressemblait à l'oreille au mot « lapin », de la même manière que l'anglais « Hobbit » était proche de « rabbit ». L'écrivain ajoute dans la même lettre qu'il n'avait jamais prévu ce rapprochement, et il met en garde les artistes contre la tentation de créer une association similaire dans leurs illustrations : « tant que les illustrateurs sont conscients que cela ne devrait pas les influencer outre mesure » (Hammond & Scull 2017, vol. 3, 451). [2]Dans la traduction de 1969, le mot « Hobbit » est conservé, mais « Hobbiton » est lu à tort comme étant proche de « Rabbiton ». Dans les traductions françaises du *Hobbit*, la carte « Les Terres Sauvages » indique donc la direction des « lapins » jusqu'en 2010 quand l'erreur est corrigée.

2. Notre traduction. Lettre datée du 15 mai 1968, issue des archives Tolkien-George Allen & Unwin chez HarperCollins.

Dans la première traduction française illustrée du Seigneur des Anneaux, en 1978, les cartes de la Terre du Milieu ne sont pas traduites.[3] Elles sont reproduites dans leur état des éditions anglaises, ce qui n'est pas le seul oubli de la traduction, comme nous l'avons souligné plus haut. Cela a pu créer une confusion chez le lectorat, qui pouvait repérer les « Dead Marshes » sur la carte sans pouvoir l'associer avec le nom donné dans le texte, « Marais des Morts ». Dans le cas de la carte du Comté[4] dans le même volume, elle est partiellement traduite : la plupart des noms sont donnés en français, mais certains sont laissés dans la langue originale. La carte du Comté montre ainsi une majorité de noms francisés, avec quelques exceptions comme « Oatbarton » ou « Rushock ». Cela semble concerner principalement les toponymes qui n'apparaissent pas dans le texte, mais plus de recherches seraient nécessaires pour l'affirmer.

Dix ans plus tard, dans l'édition du *Seigneur des Anneaux* illustrée par Philippe Munch et publiée en 1988, l'artiste redessine la carte de la Terre du Milieu et la carte du Comté. Cette fois-ci, la carte montrant l'Ouest de la Terre du Milieu à la fin du Troisième Âge est entièrement traduite. Elle apparaît à deux reprises dans le premier volume : la première entre la page de titre et le poème de l'Anneau, et la seconde à côté de la carte du Comté entre le prologue et le premier chapitre. Il est surprenant de constater que les deux cartes de la Terre du Milieu sont redessinées à partie de la version de Christopher Tolkien, et traduites, mais il ne s'agit pas de la même carte reproduite deux fois. La première, sur une double page, présente des

3. Des images sont disponibles sur le site de Tolkiendil : https://www.tolkiendil.com/tolkien/biblio/sda/editions_reliees_ledoux (consulté le 25 octobre 2021).

4. « La Comté » selon la traduction de Francis Ledoux, « le Comté » dans celle de Daniel Lauzon.

ombrages et des tons de gris. Elle montre l'entièreté de la Terre du Milieu. La seconde, quant à elle, est coupée à la latitude de la Forêt de Fangorn. Les noms y sont placés à des endroits légèrement différents. Le fond de carte semble être le même, la différence d'ombrage pouvant être due aux techniques de reproduction, mais il reste à savoir pourquoi les toponymes y ont été écrits deux fois.

Dans la nouvelle édition en français du *Seigneur des Anneaux*, publiée en trois volumes entre 2014 et 2016, et dans la nouvelle traduction du *Silmarillion*, publiée en octobre 2021, Daniel Lauzon a traduit tous les toponymes qu'il lui était possible de traduire sur les cartes, et il a également pris soin de respecter leur esthétique. Afin de reproduire la graphie de Christopher Tolkien, le traducteur s'est fait graphiste et a réutilisé la calligraphie du dessinateur, recomposant les noms français en assemblant les lettres prises ici et là dans les noms anglais. Il a partagé sur son compte Twitter une vidéo de son processus. Le résultat est une carte aux coutures invisibles, dont les noms semblent avoir été tracés directement en français, ce qui crée une édition très harmonieuse.

4 - Spécificités des illustrations françaises

Cette recherche d'harmonie guide également les choix éditoriaux opérés par l'éditeur français au cours des vingt dernières années. Auparavant, quatre éditions illustrées avaient été publiées entre 1976 et 1988 : deux *Hobbits* et deux *Seigneurs des Anneaux*. La plupart étaient en noir et blanc, avec des en-têtes de chapitres, mais le *Hobbit* de 1976 présente également des illustrations pleine page en couleur, montrant principalement les personnages et un aperçu furtif de leur environnement.

Cette édition, illustrée par l'artiste français Chica, montre sur sa couverture un Bilbo enfantin et réjoui, progressant dans une sorte de jungle aux tons de jaune, d'orange et de vert. Les illustrations à l'intérieur du volume sont proches de celles d'António Quadros pour l'édition portugaise de 1962, dans laquelle Bilbo arborait également un air enfantin, ce qui avait fortement déplu à J.R.R. Tolkien. Les illustrations de Chica offrent cependant des choix de composition intéressants, comme dans celle où Bilbo s'échappe des Montagnes de Brume : le point de vue est placé à sa verticale, au-dessus de l'entrebâillement de la porte où se tient le Hobbit devant un demi-cercle de gobelins attendant de le capturer. Sous le crayon de Chica, Gollum devient un cousin de la Créature du Lac Noir, bien que son attitude ne soit pas particulièrement effrayante. Les illustrations de Chica mettent souvent les personnages deux par deux : Bilbo et Gandalf, Bilbo et Gollum, Bilbo et un Nain émergeant d'un tonneau, etc. Cela crée un effet de miroir quand le livre s'ouvre sur une illustration pleine page en noir-et-blanc où apparaissent Bilbo et Gandalf en pied, et quand il se ferme sur une illustration très similaire des deux compagnons de route, cette fois-ci à cheval et à poney. Dans les deux images, Bilbo arbore exactement la même expression, comme si les aventures qu'il avait vécues avaient finalement eu peu d'importance.

Dans le *Hobbit* de 1983 illustré par Evelyne Drouhin, une silhouette de Hobbit en train de fumer assis dans un fauteuil se répète tous les deux ou trois chapitres. Cela équivaut au procédé littéraire par lequel Bilbo raconte sa propre histoire, bien que cela ne soit pas aussi clair dans *Le Hobbit* que dans *Le Seigneur des Anneaux*, où l'on apprend l'existence du Livre Rouge. Cependant, cela fonctionne comme un rappel visuel aux lecteurs et lectrices que le personnage principal raconte sa propre histoire. On y trouve de nombreuses autres illustrations en noir et blanc, la plupart au sein du texte ou sous forme d'en-têtes de chapitres. Quelques-unes sont reproduites en pleine page. A l'exception du *leitmotiv* de Bilbo, elles sont toutes accompagnées d'une légende en italiques, parfois une citation, plus souvent une réécriture d'un passage afin de le rendre aussi concis que possible. De manière générale, les illustrations d'Evelyne Drouhin montrent des personnages ronds et enfantins, ainsi qu'un nombre limité de décors. Le grand nombre de personnages et les légendes apportées à chaque dessin rendent cette édition très adaptée aux enfants. Bien que l'artiste ne rechigne pas à représenter la bataille finale, sa vision montre le chaos de la scène plus que sa violence. Quant à Smaug, elle ne l'illustre qu'à une reprise (à l'exception de la couverture), lorsqu'il dort, allongé sur son trésor. Elle utilise les ombres et les rehauts de façon très intéressante dans cette image, afin de montrer Bilbo, l'anneau au doigt, en train de voler une coupe : ses jambes ne sont qu'un fin trait noir sur le fond blanc, tandis que sa veste sombre se mêle aux ombres projetées par la silhouette immense de Smaug. Au premier coup d'œil, les lecteurs et lectrices le voient à peine alors qu'il se tient au premier plan.

Pour le *Seigneur des Anneaux* de 1988, Philippe Munch dessine deux illustrations par chapitre dans un style qui rappelle la bande dessinée. Ses illustrations offrent une variété de sujets, depuis les paysages naturels et urbains aux portraits en passant par les natures mortes. Il dessine avec un niveau de détail équivalent la cotte de maille d'Aragorn et les flancs de la montagne enserrant la Gorge de Helm. C'est l'un des rares artistes à ne pas s'inspirer de la vue iconique de Fendeval par J.R.R. Tolkien pour le chapitre « Nombreuses Rencontres » (il y représente Gandalf au chevet de Frodo, les deux discutant après le réveil du Hobbit). Il ne modèle pas non plus Meduseld sur l'architecture anglo-saxonne : on dirait plutôt une vision tirée des *Mille et Une Nuits*, avec ses bulbes scintillants dominant un labyrinthe de maisons aux toits plats.

Les couvertures de cette édition ne sont pas dues à Philippe Munch mais à Christian Broutin. Bien que le premier ait suivi le texte de près, les interprétations du second en sont plus distantes. Le premier volume est illustré par une créature aux dents pointues et aux yeux rouges, en forme de colline, et dont la peau est une plaine piquetée de fleurs. Le troisième livre présente une silhouette sombre, probablement un Cavalier Noir, chevauchant un animal qui ressemble à un poulet du cou au pattes, avec une tête de dinosaure. Quant au quatrième livre, il présente un Hobbit (portant des genouillères de circonstance) armé d'une épée qui émet une lueur d'un rouge tellement éclatant que l'arme s'apparente plus à un sabre laser.

A partir de 1997, les éditeurs français suivent de plus près les éditions illustrées anglaises, ce qui mène à une disparition progressive des illustrations françaises. En 2007, l'édition illustrée par Philippe Munch est republiée, mais les éditions les plus récentes sont soit les grands formats illustrés par Alan Lee, soit des éditions de poche sans illustrations. Il en va de même pour *Le Hobbit*: les éditions illustrées par des artistes français se trouvent d'occasion, mais pas dans des éditions neuves.

Le corpus illustré français est désormais dominé par Alan Lee et Ted Nasmith, tout comme dans les éditions anglaises, ce qui crée un corpus harmonieux mais de moins en moins spécifique à la France.

5 - Conclusion

Aujourd'hui, l'histoire de la réception de J.R.R. et Christopher Tolkien en France se poursuit avec la traduction à venir de

Sauron Defeated, le volume 9 de *L'Histoire de la Terre du Milieu* (à venir en 2023), mais aussi avec des projets comme « Aubusson Tisse Tolkien », qui célèbre l'amour de J.R.R. Tolkien pour l'artisanat et son talent d'artiste. Le projet complet comprend treize tentures murales et un tapis, qui reproduisent des images du légendaire ainsi que des *Lettres du Père Noël*.

Bien qu'il n'y ait pas eu de livre de J.R.R. Tolkien illustré par un(e) artiste français(e) depuis 1988, la longue histoire des traductions et des illustrations auparavant, et les efforts continus pour rendre ses manuscrits disponibles au public français, montrent le dévouement des fans et des spécialistes français envers cet auteur très anglais. En septembre 2022, Christian Bourgois éditeur a publié une nouvelle édition des *Etymologies*, sans les illustrations d'Alan Lee mais avec le dessin par Tolkien de la porte de la Moria en guise de couverture, ce qui met en lumière une fois de plus les liens étroits entre traduction et illustration dans son œuvre.

About the contributors

Eric Reinders

Eric Reinders is associate professor of Religion at Emory University. He has degrees from the University of Hull and UC-Santa Barbara. He teaches on Chinese religion, Tolkien, fortune-telling, and translation. He has published on missions, iconoclasm, and obeisance in China and on the films of Hayao Miyazaki. His monograph *Reading Tolkien in Chinese: Religion, Fantasy, and Translation* is forthcoming from Bloomsbury Press.

Helena Real

Chilean trans writer, editor, and translator, as well as a professional GM. She has received some minor literary awards in Chile, Spain, and Mexico. Her stories have been included in a number of anthologies and literary magazines, including her first short story published in English, "The Sunken Temple" in *Tales of Good Dogs* (Onyx Path Publishing, 2020). She has written for various tabletop roleplaying game companies in a freelance capacity, such as Magpie Games, Evil Hat Productions, and Angry Hamster Publishing, as well as writing some solo titles, including *The Way of the Pukona* (2018) and *Ngen Mapu* (2019)

Escritora, editora y traductora trans chilena, además de directora de juegos (DJ) profesional. Ha recibido algunos premios literarios menores en Chile, España y México. Sus historias se han incluido en varias antologías y revistas literarias, incluyendo su colección autopublicada *El espejo: Cuentos breves de fantasía* (2014). Ha escrito para varias compañías de juegos de rol como autora freelance, incluyendo Magpie Games, Evil Hat Productions y Angry Hamster Publishing además de escribir algunos títulos en solitario, incluyendo *La vía de las Pukona* (2018) y *Ngen Mapu* (2019).

Martha Celis-Mendoza

Martha Celis-Mendoza (México-Spain, Universidad Iberoamericana). Ph. D. in Hispanic Literature and M. A. in Translation, El Colegio de México. B. A. in English Literature, UNAM. Dissertation: *Función de las Canciones de Poder en la obra de J.R.R. Tolkien.* Diploma in Education of Virtues through Film, ULIA. COTE, Cambridge University. Head of the Translation Diploma Program, Universidad Iberoamericana. Lecturer in Translation and Comparative Literature (UNAM; Universidad Iberoamericana, AMETLI). Courses and papers on the life and works of J.R.R. Tolkien (The Anglo Mexican Foundation, CUIH, CENART). Book chapters and papers on Alfonso Reyes; Amparo Dávila; Mexican Women Translators; Translation Studies; Detective Stories; Shakespeare. Translator of scientific and literary texts.

Martha Celis-Mendoza (México-España, Universidad Iberoamericana Ciudad de México). Doctora en Literatura Hispánica y Maestra en Traducción, El Colegio de México. Licenciada en Letras inglesas, UNAM. Tesina: *Función de las Canciones de Poder en la obra de J.R.R. Tolkien*. Diplomado en Educación en virtudes a través del cine, ULIA. COTE, Cambridge University. Coordinadora del Diplomado en Traducción, Universidad Iberoamericana. Profesora de Traducción y Literatura Comparada (UNAM; Universidad Iberoamericana, AMETLI). Cursos y conferencias sobre la vida y obra de J.R.R. Tolkien (The Anglo Mexican Foundation, CUIH, CENART). Autora de capítulos y ponencias sobre Alfonso Reyes; Amparo Dávila; traductoras mexicanas; Traductología; relato policial; Shakespeare. Traductora de texos científicos y literarios.

Aline Esperanza Maza Vázquez

Aline Esperanza Maza Vázquez (Mexico, AMETLI) is a geophysical engineer and translator in the making. She is fluent in English, French, German, and is currently studying Korean. Collaborator of the online literary broadcast project Crónicas D&D. Avid reader, aspiring polyglot, and book collector committed to the dissemination of science and literature. Her background is in Natural Sciences, and she currently works as Assistant Editor in the journal Atmósfera from Universidad Nacional Autónoma de México (National Autonomous University of Mexico). At the moment, she is training to become a literary translator at AMETLI.

Aline Esperanza Maza Vázquez (Mexico, AMETLI) es ingeniera geofísica y traductora en ciernes. Habla con fluidez inglés, francés y alemán y actualmente estudia coreano. Colaboradora del proyecto de difusión literaria en línea Crónicas D&D. Ávida lectora, aspirante a políglota y coleccionista de libros comprometida con la divulgación de la ciencia y la literatura. Su formación es en Ciencias Naturales, y actualmente trabaja como editora asistente en la revista Atmósfera de la Universidad Nacional Autónoma de México. Cuenta con un Diplomado en Traducción de textos literarios y humanísticos por parte de AMETLI.

Sonali Chunodkar

Currently an independent researcher, Sonali Chunodkar received her M.Phil. in 2015 and Ph.D. in 2020 from the Department of English, Savitribai Phule Pune University, India. Her M.Phil. thesis was a cognitive narratological examination of how Tolkien's narrative and stylistic choices are able to achieve secondary belief through the reader's co-creative activity. Her Ph.D. dissertation attempted a Husserlian phenomenological investigation into the possibility of literary belief during the act of reading in general and that of reading Tolkien's fantasy fiction in particular. She is currently working on a paper on Tolkien's influence on mythological fantasy fiction in English in India.

Joel Merriner

Joel Merriner is an Associate Lecturer in Art History at the University of Plymouth, where he teaches modules on art historical methodologies, visual culture, and the history of book illustration. His Ph.D. explored visual alterity within late Soviet-era Central and Eastern European illustrated translations of The Lord of the Rings. Joel is currently writing a monograph on Tolkien illustration in the Soviet Bloc. His latest research focuses on the global imaginary and the interconnected nature of Tolkien book illustration, fanart and film.

Marie Bretagnolle

Marie Bretagnolle is a French doctoral student whose work focuses on the illustrations created for British and American editions of J.R.R. and Christopher Tolkien's Middle-earth texts. She is preparing her PhD under the joint supervision of Vincent Ferré, a specialist of Tolkien, and Isabelle Gadoin, specialist in text-image relationships. She has presented her work at various Tolkien Society events since 2019, and interviewed Alan Lee for the French national Library in February 2020.

Marie Bretagnolle est une doctorante française dont les travaux concernent les illustrations créées pour les éditions anglaises et américaines des textes de la Terre du Milieu par J.R.R. et Christopher Tolkien. Elle prépare sa thèse sous la direction de Vincent Ferré, spécialiste de Tolkien, et Isabelle Gadoin, spécialiste des relations texte-image. Elle a présenté son travail à l'occasion de divers évènements de la Tolkien Society depuis 2019, et s'est notamment entretenue avec Alan Lee pour la Bibliothèque nationale de France en février 2020.